CLYMER®

HONDA

125-200cc TWINS • 1965-1978

The world's finest publisher of mechanical how-to manuals

PRIMEDIA
Information Data Products

P.O. Box 12901, Overland Park, Kansas 66282-2901

COVER: Photography and 1967 Honda CB160 provided by Gary Schneider, McFarland, Wisconsin. Special thanks to the Vintage Japanese Motorcycle Club (www.vjmc.org).

TOOLS AND EQUIPMENT: K&L SUPPLY CO.

CLYMER®

Publisher Shawn Etheridge

EDITORIAL

Managing Editor
James Grooms

Associate Editors
Tom Beazley
Lee Buell

Technical Writers
Jay Bogart
Jon Engleman
Michael Morlan
George Parise
Mark Rolling
Ed Scott
Ron Wright

Editorial Production Manager
Dylan Goodwin

Senior Production Editor
Greg Araujo

Production Editors
Holly Messinger
Darin Watson

Associate Production Editors
Susan Hartington
Julie Jantzer-Ward
Justin Marciniak

Technical Illustrators
Steve Amos
Errol McCarthy
Mitzi McCarthy
Bob Meyer

MARKETING/SALES AND ADMINISTRATION

Marketing Director
Rod Cain

Manager, Promotions and Packaging
Elda Starke

Advertising & Promotions Coordinator
Melissa Abbott

Art Director
Chris Paxton

Associate Art Director
Jennifer Knight

Sales Managers
Dutch Sadler, Marine
Matt Tusken, Motorcycles

Business Manager
Ron Rogers

Customer Service Manager
Terri Cannon

Customer Service Representatives
Shawna Davis
Courtney Hollars
Susan Kohlmeyer
Jennifer Lassiter
April LeBlond

Warehouse & Inventory Manager
Leah Hicks

PRIMEDIA
Business Magazines & Media
P.O. Box 12901, Overland Park, KS 66282-2901 • 800-262-1954 • 913-967-1719

The following books and guides are published by PRIMEDIA Business Directories & Books.

More information available at *primediabooks.com*

CONTENTS

QUICK REFERENCE DATA

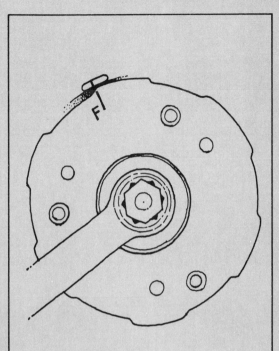

IGNITION TIMING

The "F" mark on the alternator rotor must align with the index pointer just as the ignition breaker points begin to open.

ENGINE OIL GRADE

Temperature Range	Oil Viscosity
Below 32°F	10W, 10W-30, or 10W-40
32 to 60°F	20W, 10W-30, or 10W-40
Above 60°F	30W, 10W-30, or 10W-40

CRANKCASE OIL QUANTITY

Model	Pints	Liters
125	2.5	1.2
160	3.2	1.5
175	3.2	1.5
200	3.6	1.7

CARBURETOR FLOAT HEIGHT

Model	Inches	Millimeters
125	0.93	21.0
160	0.77	19.5
CD175	1.09	28.0
All other 175 and 200 models	0.83	21.0

ADJUSTMENTS

Adjustment	Measurement
Drive chain play	¾-1 in. (20-25mm)
Front brake lever free play	3⁄16-5⁄16 in. (5-8mm)
Rear brake pedal free play	¾-1 in. (20-25mm)
Clutch lever free play	¾ in. (20mm)

TUNE-UP SPECIFICATIONS

	Inches	Millimeters
Breaker point gap	0.012-0.016	0.30-0.40
Spark plug gap	0.025-0.028	0.60-0.70
Valve clearance*	0.002	0.05

* Engine must be cold when checking valve clearance.

TIRES

Tire Size	Inflation Pressure (psi)
2.50-18	23
2.75-18	23
3.00-18	23
3.25-18	23
3.50-18	23
4.00-18	23
3.00-19	23
3.25-19	23

FORK OIL QUANTITY

Model	Ounces	Cubic Centimeters
125, 160	5.7	170
CB175, CL175	4.5-4.8	135-145
SL175	5.8-6.2	175-185
200	4.3-4.5	128-132

- NOTES -

CHAPTER ONE

GENERAL INFORMATION

This manual provides maintenance and repair information for all of the Honda twins listed on the back cover.

MANUAL ORGANIZATION

This chapter provides general information and discusses equipment and tools useful for preventive maintenance and troubleshooting.

Chapter Two explains lubrication and maintenance procedures necessary to keep your motorcycle running right, plus a complete tune-up section.

Chapter Three provides methods and suggestions for quick and accurate diagnosis and repair of problems. Troubleshooting procedures discuss typical symptoms and methods to pinpoint the trouble.

Chapter Four offers complete repair procedures for all Honda twin-cylinder engines.

Subsequent chapters describe specific systems such as fuel and exhaust systems; electrical system; and frame, suspension, and steering.

Each chapter provides disassembly, repair, and assembly procedures in simple step-by-step form. If a repair is impractical for a home mechanic, it is so indicated. It is usually faster and less expensive to take such repairs to a dealer or competent repair shop.

Throughout this manual keep in mind two conventions: "front" refers to the front of the motorcycle. The front of any component such as the engine is that end which faces toward the front of the motorcycle. The left and right sides refer to a person sitting on the motorcycle facing forward.

The terms NOTE, CAUTION, and WARNING have specific meanings in this manual. A NOTE provides additional information to make a step or procedure easier or clearer. Disregarding a NOTE could cause inconvenience, but would not cause damage or personal injury.

A CAUTION emphasizes areas where equipment damage could result. Disregarding a CAUTION could cause permanent mechanical damage; however, personal injury is unlikely.

A WARNING emphasizes areas where personal injury or even death could result from negligence. Mechanical damage may also occur. WARNINGS *are to be taken seriously*. In some cases serious injury or death has resulted from disregarding similar warnings.

The use of special tools has been kept to a minimum. Where special tools are required, illustrations are provided. The resourceful mechanic can, in many cases, improvise with acceptable substitutes — there is always another way. If a substitute is used, however, care should be exercised so as not to damage parts.

SERVICE HINTS

Most of the service procedures covered are straightforward and can be performed by anyone reasonably handy with tools. It is suggested, however, that you consider your own capabilities carefully before attempting any operation involving major disassembly of the engine.

Some operations, for example, require the use of a press. It would be wiser to have these performed by a shop equipped for such work, rather than trying to do the job yourself with makeshift equipment. Other procedures require precision measurements. Unless you have the skills and equipment to make these measurements, call on a competent service outlet.

You will find that repairs will go much faster and easier if your machine is clean before you begin work. There are special cleaners for washing the engine and related parts. You just brush or spray on the cleaning solution, let it stand, and rinse it away with a garden hose. Clean all oily or greasy parts with cleaning solvent as you remove them.

WARNING
Never use gasoline as a cleaning agent. Gasoline presents an extreme fire hazard. Be sure to work in a well-ventilated area when you use cleaning solvent of any kind. Keep a fire extinguisher handy, just in case.

Special tools are required for some service procedures. These tools may be purchased at Honda dealers. If you are on good terms with the dealer's service department, you may be able to use their tools.

Much of the labor charge for repairs made by dealers is for removal and disassembly of other parts in order to reach the defective one. It is frequently possible for you to do all of this yourself, then take the affected subassembly into the dealer for repair.

Once you decide to tackle the job yourself, read the engine section in this manual which pertains to the job. Study the illustrations and the text until you have a good idea of what is in- volved. If special tools are required, make arrangements to get them before you start the job. It is frustrating to get partly into a job and find that you are unable to complete it.

TOOLS

Every motorcyclist should carry a small tool kit with him, to help make minor roadside adjustments and repairs.

For more extensive servicing, an assortment of ordinary hand tools is required. As a minimum, have the following available.

 a. Combination wrenches (metric)
 b. Socket wrenches (metric)
 c. Assorted screwdrivers
 d. Assorted pliers
 e. Spark plug gauge
 f. Spark plug wrench
 g. Small hammer
 h. Plastic mallet
 i. Parts cleaning brush

A few special tools may also be required. The first four are essential.

Ignition Gauge

This tool combines round wire spark plug gap gauges with narrow breaker point feeler gauges. The device costs about $3 at auto accessory stores. See **Figure 1**.

Compression Gauge

An engine with low compression cannot be properly tuned and will not develop full power. A compression gauge measures engine compression. The one shown in **Figure 2** has a flexible stem, which enables it to reach cylinders where there is little clearance between the cylinder head and frame. Inexpensive gauges start at around $3, and are available at auto accessory stores or by mail order.

Impact Driver

This tool might have been designed with the motorcycle mechanic in mind. It makes removal of engine cover screws easy, and eliminates damaged screw slots. Good ones run

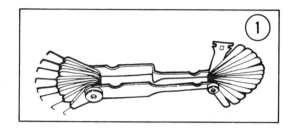

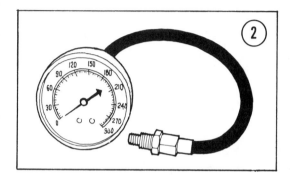

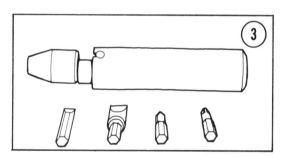

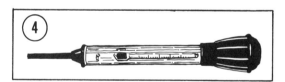

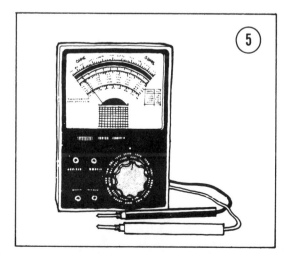

about $12 at larger hardware stores. See **Figure 3**.

Hydrometer

This instrument measures state of charge of the battery, and tells much about battery condition. Such an instrument is available at any auto parts store and through most larger mail order outlets. Satisfactory ones cost as little as $3. See **Figure 4**.

Multimeter or VOM

This instrument is invaluable for electrical system troubleshooting and service. A few of its functions may be duplicated by locally fabricated substitutes, but for the serious hobbyist, it is a must. See **Figure 5**.

EXPENDABLE SUPPLIES

Certain expendable supplies are also required. These include grease, oil, gasket cement, wiping rags, cleaning solvent, and distilled water. Cleaning solvent is available at many service stations. Distilled water, required for battery service, is available at every supermarket.

MECHANIC'S TIPS

Removing Frozen Nuts and Screws

When a fastener rusts and cannot be removed, several methods may be used to loosen it. First apply penetrating oil liberally. Rap the fastener several times with a small hammer; don't hit it hard enough to cause damage.

For frozen screws, apply oil as described, then insert a screwdriver in the slot and rap the top of the screwdriver with a hammer. This loosens the rust so the screw can be removed in the normal way. If the screw head is too chewed up to use a screwdriver, grip the head with vise-type pliers and turn the screw out.

For a frozen bolt or nut, apply penetrating oil, then rap it with a hammer. Turn off with the proper size wrench. If the points are rounded off, grip with vise-type pliers as described for screws.

Stripped Threads

Occasionally, threads are stripped through carelessness or impact damage. Often the threads can be cleaned up by running a tap (for internal threads) or die (for external threads) through the threads. See **Figure 6**.

Broken Screw or Bolt

When the head breaks off a screw or bolt, several methods are available for removing the remaining portion.

If a large portion of the remainder projects out, try gripping it with vise-type pliers. If the projection portion is too small, try filing it to fit a wrench or cut a slot in it to fit a screwdriver. See **Figure 7**.

If the head breaks off flush, as it usually does, remove it with a screw extractor. Refer to **Figure 8**. Center-punch the broken part, then drill a hole into it. Drill sizes are marked on the tool. Tap the extractor into the broken part, then back it out with a wrench.

Removing Damaged Screws

WARNING
When removing screws by this method, always wear suitable eye protection.

CAUTION
Use clean rags to cover bearings or any other parts which might be harmed by metal chips produced during this procedure.

Figure 9 illustrates damaged screws typical of those on many bikes. Such screws may usually be removed easily by drilling. Select a bit with a diameter larger than that of the damaged screw, but smaller than its head, then drill into the screw head **(Figure 10)** until the head separates from the screw. The remainder of the screw may then be turned out easily. **Figure 11** illustrates one screw head removed in this manner. The other has been drilled to just the point where the head is separating from the screw body. Note that there is no damage to the plate which these screws retain.

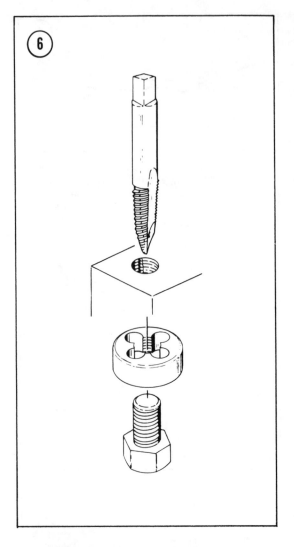

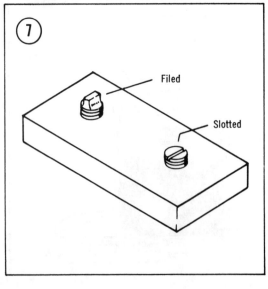

1

⑧

REMOVING BROKEN SCREWS AND BOLTS

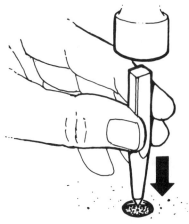

1. Center punch broken stud

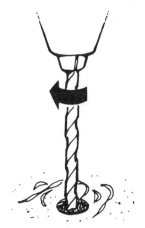

2. Drill hole in stud

3. Tap in screw extractor

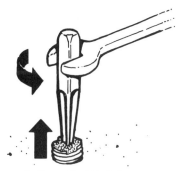

4. Remove broken stud

⑨ ⑩

SAFETY FIRST

Professional mechanics can work for years without sustaining serious injury. If you observe a few rules of common sense and safety, you can also enjoy many safe hours servicing your own machine. You can also hurt yourself or damage the bike if you ignore these rules:

1. Never use gasoline as a cleaning solvent.

2. Never smoke or use a torch near flammable liquids, such as cleaning solvent in open containers.

3. Never smoke or use a torch in an area where batteries are charging. Highly explosive hydrogen gas is formed during the charging process.

4. If welding or brazing is required on the machine, remove the fuel tank to a safe distance, at least 50 feet away.

5. Be sure to use proper size wrenches for nut turning.

6. If a nut is tight, think for a moment what would happen to your hand should the wrench slip. Be guided accordingly.

7. Keep your work area clean and uncluttered.

8. Wear safety goggles in all operations involving drilling, grinding, or use of a chisel.

9. Never use worn tools.

10. Keep a fire extinguisher handy. Be sure that it is rated for gasoline and electrical fires.

CHAPTER TWO

LUBRICATION AND MAINTENANCE

To gain the utmost in safety, performance, and useful life from your motorcycle, it is necessary to make periodic inspections and adjustments. It frequently happens that minor problems found during such inspections are simple and inexpensive to correct at the time, but could lead to major failures later. This chapter describes such services.

Table 1 is a suggested maintenance schedule.

Table 1   MAINTENANCE SCHEDULE

Maintenance Item	Miles 1,000	3,000	6,000
Engine tune-up		X	
Check battery	X		
Change oil	X	X	X
Service oil filter			X
Adjust clutch		X	
Check lights and horn	X		
Adjust chain	X		
Adjust brakes	X		
Check brake lining			X
Check wheels	X		
Check tires	X		
Change fork oil		X	
Grease wheel bearings			X
Check steering bearings			X
Grease swing arm		X	

ENGINE TUNE-UP

The purpose of a tune-up is to restore power and performance lost over a gradual period of time due to normal wear.

Carry out the tune-up in the same sequence as in this chapter for best results.

Cam Chain Adjustment

Engine valves and breaker points are opened and closed by a chain-driven camshaft. Wear in this chain results in altered valve and ignition timing, so it is necessary to adjust chain tension periodically. Refer to **Figure 1** for the following steps.

1. Loosen locknut, then slightly loosen bolt. The cam chain slack will be taken up automatically by spring pressure.

2. Tighten bolt, then hold it in place and tighten locknut.

Valve Adjustment

Valves must be adjusted while the engine is cold.

1. Remove the alternator cover (**Figure 2**).

2. Remove all tappet covers (**Figure 3**).

3. Turn the engine over until the T mark on the alternator rotor aligns with its index pointer (**Figure 4**).

4. Check both cylinders to see which one has both valves closed. Adjust the valves on that cylinder as follows (refer to **Figure 5** for the following procedure):

   a. Loosen locknut, then turn valve adjuster as required to adjust clearance between valve stem and adjuster screw. Clearance should be 0.002 in. (0.05mm) for each valve.

   b. Tighten the locknut and recheck the adjustment. Readjust if necessary.

   c. Turn engine one complete turn, then repeat Steps 3-4 for remaining cylinder.

   d. Install tappet covers (refer to **Figure 3**) and alternator cover (refer to **Figure 2**).

Compression Test

An engine requires adequate compression to develop full power. If for any reason compression is low, the engine will not develop full power. A compression test, or even better, a series of them over the life of the motorcycle, will tell much about engine condition.

To carry out a compression test, proceed as follows:

1. Start the engine, then ride the bike long enough to warm it thoroughly.

2. Remove each spark plug (refer to *Spark Plug Inspection and Service*, following section).

3. Screw a compression gauge into the spark plug hole, or if a press-in type gauge is used, hold it firmly in position (**Figure 6**).

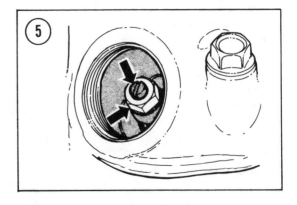

4. With the ignition switch OFF, and the throttle wide open, crank the engine briskly with the kickstarter several times; the compression gauge indication will increase with each kick. Continue to crank the engine until the gauge shows no more increase, then record the gauge indication. For example, on the first kick the gauge might indicate 90 psi; the second kick, 140 psi; the third kick, 160 psi, etc.

5. Repeat this procedure for the remaining cylinder. Normal compression pressure at sea level will be about 140-170 psi, decreasing with altitude.

A sudden drop in cylinder compression could be caused by many factors, most of which require major engine service. Some of these causes are worn piston rings, a leaking cylinder head gasket, or a leaking valve.

A quick check for worn piston rings is easy: pour a spoonful of heavy engine oil through the spark plug opening. The oil will flow over the head of the piston, temporarily sealing the piston rings. Repeat the compression test for that cylinder. If compression comes up to normal (or near normal), it is an indication that the rings are worn, or the cylinder defective.

If compression remains low after pouring oil into the spark plug hole and repeating the compression test, it is likely that a valve or head gasket is leaking. (A rapid on-off squeal when the engine is running, frequently accompanies this condition.)

On Honda twins, a difference of 25% in compression measurements between cylinders should be taken as an indication that engine repairs should be made. Likewise, a difference of 25% between successive measurements on any cylinder over a period of time (if made under identical conditions) is also an indication of trouble.

Table 2 may be used as a quick reference when checking cylinder compression pressures. It has been calculated so that the lowest reading number is 75% of the highest reading number. *Example:* After checking the compression pressures in all cylinders it was found that the highest pressure obtained was 150 psi. The lowest pressure reading was 140 psi. By locating 150 in the maximum column, it is seen that the minimum allowable pressure is 113. Since the lowest reading obtained was 140 psi, the compression is within satisfactory limits.

Table 2   COMPRESSION PRESSURE LIMITS

Pressure (psi)		Pressure (psi)	
Maximum	Minimum	Maximum	Minimum
134	101	188	141
136	102	190	142
138	104	192	144
140	105	194	145
142	107	196	147
146	110	198	148
148	111	200	150
150	113	202	151
152	114	204	153
154	115	206	154
156	117	208	156
158	118	210	157
160	120	212	158
162	121	214	160
164	123	216	162
166	124	218	163
168	126	220	165
170	127	222	166
172	129	224	168
174	131	226	169
176	132	228	171
178	133	230	172
180	135	232	174
182	136	234	175
184	138	236	177
186	140	238	178

Spark Plug Inspection and Service

Spark plugs are available in various heat ranges hotter or colder than the spark plug originally installed at the factory.

Select plugs of a heat range designed for the loads and temperature conditions under which the engine will run. Use of incorrect heat ranges can cause seized pistons, scored cylinder walls, or damaged piston crowns.

In general, use a low-numbered plug for low speeds, low loads, and low temperatures. Use a higher-numbered plug for high speeds, high engine loads, and high temperatures.

> NOTE: *Use the highest numbered plug that will not foul. In areas where seasonal temperature variations are great, the factory recommends a high-numbered plug for slower winter operation.*

The reach (length) of a plug is also important. A longer-than-normal plug could interfere with the piston, causing severe damage. Refer to **Figures 7 and 8**.

Spark plugs of the correct heat range, with the engine in a proper state of tune, will appear light tan. See **Figure 9** for the various spark plug conditions you might encounter.

Changing spark plugs is generally a simple operation. Occasionally heat and corrosion can cause the plug to bind in the cylinder head, making removal difficult. Do not use force; the head is easily damaged. The proper way to replace a plug is described in the following steps.

1. Blow out any debris which has collected in the spark plug wells. It could fall into the hole and cause damage.

2. Gently remove the spark plug leads by pulling up and out on the cap. Do not jerk or pull on the wire itself.

3. Apply penetrating oil to the base of the plug and allow it to work into the threads.

4. Back out the plugs with a socket that has a rubber insert designed to grip the insulator. Be careful not to drop the plugs where they could become lodged.

> NOTE: *Be sure that you remember which cylinder each spark plug came out of. The condition of the spark plug is an indication of engine condition and can warn of developing trouble that can be isolated by cylinder (refer to **Figure 9**).*

5. Remove the spark plug gaskets from the spark plug holes. Clean the seating area after

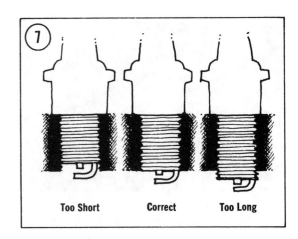

Too Short   Correct   Too Long

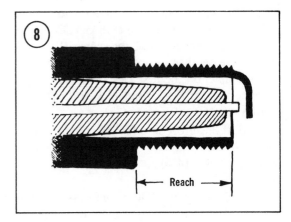

← Reach →

removal, being careful that dirt does not drop into the spark plug hole.

6. Remove grease and dirt from the insulator with a clean rag. Inspect the insulator and body of each spark plug for signs of cracks and chips. Replace if defective.

> NOTE: *If one plug is found unsatisfactory, replace both of them.*

7. Clean the tips of the plugs with a sandblasting machine (some gas stations have them) or a wire brush and solvent.

8. File the center electrode flat. Clean and file all surfaces of the outer electrode. All surfaces should be clean, flat, and smooth.

9. Use a round feeler gauge and adjust the clearance between the electrodes as specified in **Table 3**. See **Figure 10**.

> CAUTION
> *Do not bend the inner electrode or damage to the insulator may result.*

9

2

Normal plug appearance noted by the brown to grayish-tan deposits and slight electrode wear. This plug indicates the correct plug heat range and proper air fuel ratio.

Red, brown, yellow and white coatings caused by fuel and oil additives. These deposits are not harmful if they remain in a powdery form.

Carbon fouling distinguished by dry, fluffy black carbon deposits which may be caused by an over-rich air/fuel mixture, excessive hand choking, clogged air filter or excessive idling.

Shiny yellow glaze on insulator cone is caused when the powdery deposits from fuel and oil additives melt. Melting occurs during hard acceleration after prolonged idling. This glaze conducts electricity and shorts out the plug.

Oil fouling indicated by wet, oily deposits caused by oil pumping past worn rings or down the intake valve guides. A hotter plug temporarily reduces oil deposits, but a plug that is too hot leads to pre-ignition and possible engine damage.

Overheated plug indicated by burned or blistered insulator tip and badly worn electrodes. This condition may be caused by pre-ignition, cooling system defects, lean air/fuel ratios, low octane fuel or over advanced ignition timing.

Spark plug condition photos courtesy of AC Spark Plug Division, General Motors Corporation.

10. Use a new gasket if the old plugs are to be reused after cleaning. Apply a dab of graphite to the spark plug threads to simplify future removal.

11. Thread the plugs into the spark plug holes finger-tight, then tighten ¼ turn more with a wrench. Further tightening will flatten the gasket and cause binding. (If a torque wrench is available, tighten spark plugs to 15 ft.-lb.)

Breaker Points

Normal use of a motorcycle causes the breaker points to burn and pit gradually. If they are not pitted too badly, they can be dressed with a few strokes of a clean point file or Flex-stone.

CAUTION

Do not use emery cloth or sandpaper to dress the points as particles can remain on the points and cause arcing and burning.

If a few strokes of the file do not smooth the points completely, replace them.

Oil or dirt may get on the points, resulting in poor performance or even premature failure. Common causes for this condition are defective oil seals, improper or excessive breaker cam lubrication, or lack of care when the breaker point cover is removed.

Points should be cleaned and regapped every 1,500-2,000 miles (2,000-3,000 kilometers). To clean the points, first dress them lightly with a clean point file, then remove all residue with lacquer thinner. Close the points on a piece of clean white paper (such as a business card). Continue to pull the card through the closed points until no discoloration or residue remains on the card. Finally, rotate the engine and observe the points as they open and close. If they do not meet squarely, replace them.

To adjust the points, proceed as follows.

1. Remove breaker point cover (**Figure 11**).

2. Remove the alternator cover (**Figure 12**) and turn engine over until the points are open to the maximum gap.

3. Measure the breaker point gap with a feeler gauge (**Figure 13**). Point gap should be 0.012-

Table 3   SPARK PLUG GAP

Model	Inches	Millimeters
125-200	0.025-0.028	0.60-0.70

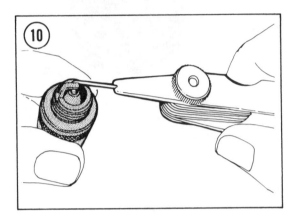

0.016 in. (0.30-0.40mm). If so, go on to Step 7. If adjustment is necessary, continue with Step 4.

4. Slightly loosen the base plate retaining screws. Refer to **Figure 14**.

5. Move the base plate until the point gap is 0.014 in. (0.35mm) as shown in **Figure 14**.

6. Tighten both base plate retaining screws, then check gap again. Readjust if necessary.

7. Perform the preceding steps when the points are fully open on the remaining lobe of the contact breaker cam (in order to adjust the breaker point gap for the other cylinder).

8. Wipe the breaker cam clean, then apply a very small quantity of breaker cam lubricant. Apply just enough to create an oil film on the cam; more may cause point failure. This lubricant is sold at any auto parts store.

9. Adjust ignition timing (refer to *Ignition Timing*, following section).

To replace breaker points, disconnect wire which is attached to the movable contact, then remove both retaining screws (refer to **Figure 14**). Be sure to adjust point gap and ignition timing after installation.

Ignition Timing

Any change in breaker point gap, either from normal wear or from breaker point service, affects ignition timing. If spark plugs fire too

early, severe engine damage may result. Over-heating and loss of power will occur if the spark occurs too late.

1. Remove the breaker point cover and alternator cover (refer to **Figures 11 and 12**).

2. Place a wrench on the alternator bolt and turn the engine over until the F mark on the alternator rotor aligns with the index pointer (**Figure 15**).

3. Connect a timing tester to the breaker point terminal and a good ground (follow the manu-

facturer's hook-up instructions). If no timing tester is available, make up a test lamp as shown in **Figure 16**.

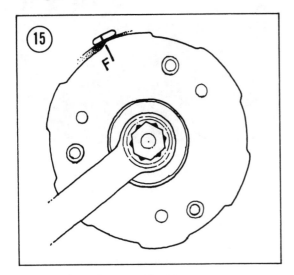

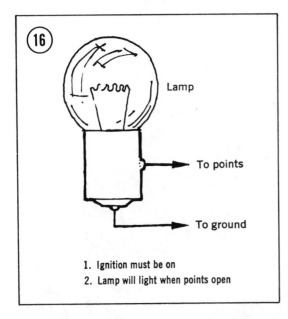

Lamp

→ To points

→ To ground

1. Ignition must be on
2. Lamp will light when points open

4. Loosen both base plate retaining screws (refer to **Figure 14**) just enough so that the base plate can be moved slightly. Turn the base plate gradually until the points just begin to open (if a test lamp is used to determine point opening, be sure that the ignition switch is ON). The test lamp will light exactly at the moment that the F mark on the alternator rotor aligns with the index pointer, if the ignition timing is correct (**Figure 17**).

5. Tighten the base plate retaining screws.

6. Recheck adjustment by turning the rotor clockwise slightly, then counterclockwise slowly. The F mark and index should align just as the points open (and the test lamp lights up). Readjust if necessary.

7. To check the remaining cylinder, turn the rotor one full revolution (360 degrees) and perform the preceding steps again.

Air Cleaner Service

During the tune-up, the air cleaner element should be cleaned or replaced.

1. Remove the clamps and retaining nuts and lift the air cleaner off (**Figures 18 and 19**).

2. Remove the element and tap it gently against the palm of your hand to dislodge dirt from the outside. Then blow compressed air gently from the inside. Replace a damaged element, or one that is too dirty to clean satisfactorily.

3. Install by reversing the preceding steps.

Carburetor Adjustment

1. Start engine and allow to warm to operating temperature, then shut it off.

2. Turn each idle mixture screw in until it seats lightly, then back out each one 1¼ turns (**Figure 20**).

3. Start the engine. Adjust each idle speed screw so that the engine idles at 1,000-2,000 rpm (**Figure 21**).

4. Place one hand behind each muffler and adjust idle speed screw (refer to **Figure 21**) until exhaust pressure from each muffler is equal.

5. Turn left cylinder idle mixture screw in either direction, slowly, until engine idle speed is at its maximum.

6. Repeat Step 5 for the right cylinder.

7. Check exhaust pressure from each cylinder (as in Step 4) and adjust either idle speed screw necessary to equalize pressures.

8. Turn each idle speed screw an equal amount to obtain 1,000-1,200 rpm idle speed.

9. Synchronize both carburetors (refer to last procedure, this section).

If the preceding procedure does not work well, due to both carburetors being too far out of adjustment, use the following procedure:

1. Turn the idle mixture screw on each carburetor in until it seats lightly, then back it out 1¼ turns (refer to **Figure 20**).

2. Start the engine, then ride the bike long enough to warm it thoroughly.

3. Stop the engine and disconnect either spark plug lead.

4. Restart the engine on one cylinder. Turn the idle speed screw on the "working" carburetor in enough to keep the engine running (refer to **Figure 21**).

5. Turn the idle speed screw out until the engine runs slower and begins to falter.

6. Turn the idle mixture screw in or out to make the engine run smoothly. Note the speed indicated by the tachometer.

7. Repeat Steps 5 and 6 to achieve the lowest possible stable idle speed.

8. Stop the engine, then reconnect the spark plug lead that was disconnected.

9. Repeat Steps 3 through 8 for the other cylinder, matching the engine speed with that observed in Step 6.

10. Start the engine, then turn each idle speed screw an equal amount until the engine idles at 1,000-1,200 rpm.

11. Place one hand behind each muffler and check that the exhaust pressures are equal. If not, turn either idle speed screw in or out until they are equal.

12. Adjust carburetor synchronization (see following procedure).

To synchronize the carburetors, proceed as follows:

1. Twist the throttle grip and see if both throttle slides begin to move upward at the same time (**Figure 22**).

> NOTE: *A small mirror may be helpful during this check.*

2. If throttle slides need adjusting, turn the cable adjuster at the top of either carburetor until the slides move together perfectly (**Figure 23**).

CLUTCH ADJUSTMENT

Adjust the clutch at 1,000-mile (1,500-kilometer) intervals.

1. Refer to **Figure 24**. Loosen locknut, then turn cable adjuster until cable is all the way into the clutch lever bracket.
2. Refer to **Figure 25**. Loosen locknut (A), then turn cable adjuster (B) in direction shown to fully loosen the cable.
3. Refer to **Figure 26**. Loosen locknut or bolt (B), turn adjuster screw counterclockwise until it meets resistance. Turn clockwise 1/4 turn, then tighten locknut or bolt.
4. Refer to **Figure 25**. Turn lower cable adjuster so that there is approximately 3/4 in. (20 mm) free play at the clutch hand lever, then tighten lower cable adjuster locknut.
5. Tighten upper cable adjuster locknut. Minor adjustments can then be made at the upper cable adjuster.

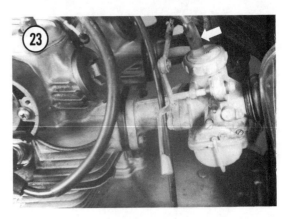

BRAKES

Drum brakes are standard on the rear of all Honda Twins covered in this manual. Some models use a mechanically-actuated front disc brake; others use a drum brake.

Adjust brakes every 1,000 miles (1,500 kilometers), or whenever necessary.

Front (Disc) Brake Adjustment

The front disc brake is self-adjusting and needs no periodic maintenance other than brake pad replacement.

Front (Drum) Brake Adjustment

To adjust the front drum brake, refer to **Figure 27**.

1. Support the motorcycle so that its front wheel is free to turn.
2. Loosen locknut.
3. Turn adjuster nut to obtain desired braking action.
4. Tighten locknut.

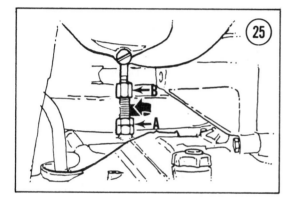

Rear (Drum) Brake Adjustment

The rear drum brake is operated by a rod. Simply turn the adjusting nut (**Figure 28**) until the rear brake pedal has approximately ¾-1 in. (20-25mm) of free play.

STEERING STEM BEARINGS

Check steering bearings for looseness or binding. *If any exists, find out the cause and correct it immediately.* Refer to Chapter Seven, *Steering Stem* section, for repair procedures.

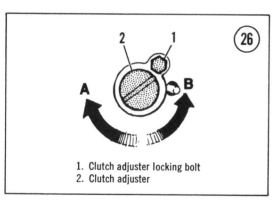

1. Clutch adjuster locking bolt
2. Clutch adjuster

Adjustment

1. Remove steering stem nut (**Figure 29**).

2. Loosen pinch bolt, then tighten or loosen the ring nut by tapping it gently with a suitable drift until the steering stem turns freely throughout its full travel without excessive looseness or binding (**Figure 30**). Tighten the pinch bolt securely.

3. Tighten the steering stem nut securely (refer to **Figure 29**).

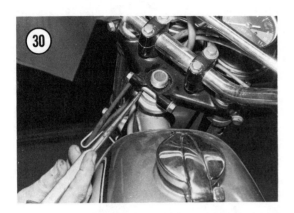

WHEELS AND TIRES

Check wheels for bent rims and loose or missing spokes. Complete wheel inspection and service procedures are detailed in Chapter Seven, *Wheels* section.

Check tires for worn treads, cuts, and proper inflation. Refer to **Table 4**.

BATTERY

The battery should always be clean and the cells filled (but not overfilled) with distilled water. Most batteries are marked with electrolyte level limit lines. Always maintain the fluid level between these two lines. (Distilled water is available at most supermarkets.)

Overfilling leads to loss of electrolyte, resulting in poor battery performance, short life, and excessive corrosion. Never allow the electrolyte level to fall below the top of the battery plates, as the plates could become permanently damaged due to contact with the air.

Excessive battery water consumption is an indication that the battery is being overcharged. The two most common causes of overcharging are high battery temperature or high voltage regulator setting.

> **WARNING**
> *When working with batteries, use extreme care to avoid spilling or splashing electrolyte. This electrolyte is sulfuric acid, which can destroy clothing and cause serious chemical burns. Neutralize spilled battery acid immediately with a solution of baking soda and water, then flush away with clean water.*

> *Safety glasses should be worn when working near a battery, to avoid having electrolyte splashed into the eyes. If electrolyte comes into contact with the eyes, force eyes open and flood with cool, clean water for about 5 minutes, and call a physician immediately.*

Battery Charging

> **WARNING**
> *When batteries are being charged, highly explosive gas forms in each cell. Some of this gas escapes through the filler openings and may form an explosive atmosphere around the battery (which may last for several hours). Keep sparks, open flame, or lighted cigarettes away from a battery under charge, or in a room where one has been recently charged. A common cause of battery explosions is the disconnection of a live circuit at a battery terminal (a spark usually occurs under these conditions). To avoid this, be sure that the power switch is off before making or breaking connections. (Poor connections are also a common cause of electrical arcs which cause explosions.)*

Motorcycle batteries are not designed for high charge or discharge rates. For this reason, it is recommended that a motorcycle battery be charged at a rate not exceeding 10% of its ampere-hour capacity.

Example: Do not exceed 0.5 ampere charging rate for a 5 ampere-hour battery, or 1.5 amperes for a 15 ampere-hour battery.

Table 4   TIRE INFLATION

Tire Size	Inflation Pressure (psi)
2.50-18	23
2.75-18	23
3.00-18	23
3.25-18	23
3.50-18	23
4.00-18	23
3.00-19	23
3.25-19	23

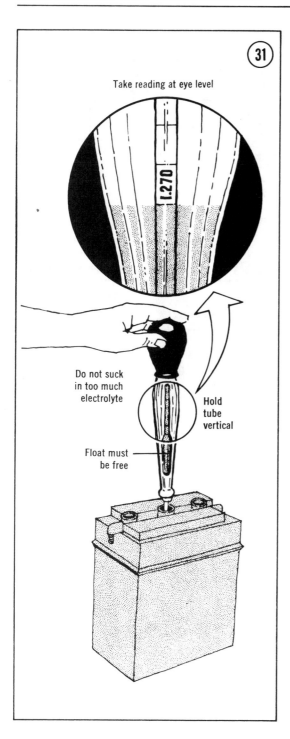

Take reading at eye level

1.270

Do not suck in too much electrolyte

Hold tube vertical

Float must be free

will not perform as well as it should, but it may continue to provide satisfactory service for a time.

Some temperature rise is normal as a battery is being charged. Do not allow electrolyte temperature to exceed 110 degrees F. Should temperature reach that figure, discontinue charging until the battery cools, then resume charging at a lower rate.

Testing State of Charge

Place the tube of a hydrometer into the filler opening and draw in just enough electrolyte to lift the float (**Figure 31**). Hold the instrument in a vertical position and read specific gravity on the scale, where the float stem emerges from the electrolyte.

Specific gravity of the electrolyte varies with temperature, so it is necessary to apply a temperature correction to the reading so obtained. For each 10 degrees that battery temperature exceeds 80 degrees F, add 0.004 to the indicated specific gravity. Likewise, subtract 0.004 from the indicated value for each 10 degrees that battery temperature is below 80 degrees F.

Repeat this measurement for each battery cell. If there is more than 0.050 difference (50 points) between cells, battery condition is questionable.

State of charge may be determined from **Figure 32**.

Do not measure specific gravity immediately after adding water. Ride the machine a few miles to ensure thorough mixture of the electrolyte.

It is most important to maintain batteries fully charged during cold weather. A fully charged battery freezes at a much lower temperature than one which is partially discharged. Freezing temperature depends on specific gravity. Refer to **Table 5**.

This charge rate should continue for 10 hours if the battery is completely discharged, or until specific gravity of each cell is up to 1.260-1.280, corrected for temperature. If after prolonged charging, specific gravity of one or more cells does not come up to at least 1.230, the battery

Battery Cables

Keep battery cables tight and clean (free of corrosion, grease, etc.). If the cables are corroded, disconnect them and clean them separately with a wire brush and a baking soda and

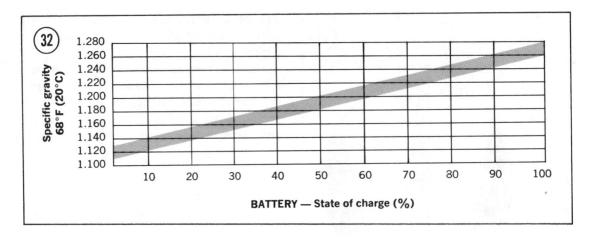

water solution. After cleaning, apply a thin coating of petroleum jelly to the battery terminals before installing the cables. After connecting the cables, apply a light coating to the connection. This procedure will help to prevent future corrosion.

DRIVE CHAIN

Clean, lubricate, and adjust the drive chain every 1,000 miles (1,500 kilometers), or whenever necessary. The drive chain becomes worn after prolonged use. Wear in pins, bushings, and rollers causes chain stretch. Sliding action between roller surfaces and sprocket teeth also contributes to wear.

Cleaning and Adjustment

1. Disconnect the master link (**Figure 33**) and remove chain.

2. Clean chain thoroughly with solvent.

3. Rinse chain with clean solvent, then blow dry with compressed air.

4. Examine chain carefully for wear or damage. Replace if there is any doubt as to its condition. If chain is okay, lubricate by soaking in oil, or any of the special chain lubricants available in any motorcycle shop.

5. Install the chain. Be sure master link is installed as shown in **Figure 33**.

6. Refer to **Figure 34**. Proceed with chain adjustment, as follows:

    a. Remove cotter pin and loosen rear axle nut.

Table 5   SPECIFIC GRAVITY/FREEZING TEMPERATURE

Specific Gravity	Freezing Temperature Degrees F
1.100	18
1.120	13
1.140	8
1.160	1
1.180	−6
1.200	−17
1.220	−31
1.240	−50
1.260	−75
1.280	−92

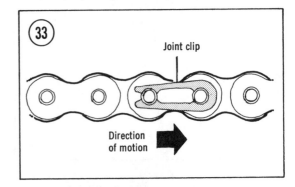

    b. Loosen locknut on each side.

    c. There is one adjustment bolt on each side. Turn it until there is ¾-1 in. (20-25mm) of up-and-down movement in the center of the lower chain run (**Figure 35**).

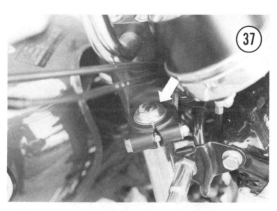

d. Be sure that the reference marks on the swinging arm and the index mark on the chain adjuster (refer to **Figure 34**) are in the same relative positions on each side.

7. Tighten the rear axle nut, then install a new cotter pin (refer to **Figure 34**).

8. Adjust the rear brake (refer to *Brakes* section, this chapter).

FORK OIL

Replacement

Replace the fork oil every 3,000 miles (4,500 kilometers), as follows:

1. Place a pan under each fork leg, then remove drain plug at lower end of each fork leg (**Figure 36**). Allow oil to drain out into pan.

> NOTE: *To aid in removing all of the oil, push down on the forks several times to force oil out.*

2. Install drain plugs, then remove upper fork bolts (**Figure 37**). Pour fresh fork oil into forks (refer to **Table 6** for fork oil quantities).

3. Install upper fork bolts.

Table 6   FORK OIL QUANTITY

Model	Ounces	Cubic Centimeters
125	5.7	170
160	5.7	170
CB175, CL175	4.5-4.8	135-145
SL175	5.8-6.2	175-185
200	4.3-4.5	128-132

OIL AND OIL FILTER

Probably the single most important maintenance item which contributes to long engine life is that of regular oil changes. Engine oil becomes contaminated with products of combustion, condensation, and dirt. Some of these contaminants react with oil, forming acids which attack vital engine components, and thereby result in premature wear.

To change engine oil, ride the bike until it is thoroughly warm, then place a pan under the engine and remove the engine oil drain plug

(**Figure 38**). Allow the oil to drain thoroughly (it may help to rock the motorcycle from side to side, and also forward and backward, to get as much oil out as possible).

Install the engine oil drain plug and refill with fresh engine oil. Refer to **Tables 8 and 9** for specifications.

Be sure to check for leaks after the oil change is completed.

Maintain the engine oil level between both level marks on the dipstick (**Figure 39**).

> NOTE: *The dipstick should not be screwed into the engine when checking oil level.*

All models are equipped with a centrifugal oil filter which separates sludge and other foreign particles from the engine oil before it is distributed throughout the engine. To clean the filter, proceed as follows:

1. Remove oil filter cover (**Figure 40**).

2. Remove internal circlip holding oil filter cap (**Figure 41**).

3. Remove oil filter cap (**Figure 42**).

4. Clean cap in solvent and install with a new O-ring. Secure with internal circlip (refer to **Figure 41**).

5. Install oil filter cover with a new gasket (refer to **Figure 40**). Use a sealer such as Gasgacinch.

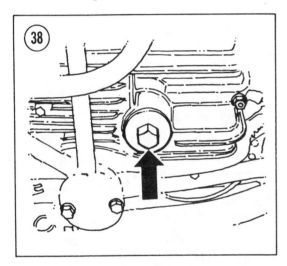

Table 7   OIL GRADE

Temperature Range	Oil Grade
Below 32°F	10W, 10W-30, or 10W-40
32 to 60°F	20W, 10W-30, or 10W-40
Above 60°F	30W, 10W-30, or 10W-40

Table 8   REFILL QUANTITY

Model	Pints	Liters
125	2.5	1.2
160	3.2	1.5
175	3.2	1.5
200	3.6	1.7

SWINGING ARM

Disassemble the swinging arm and grease its pivot shaft and bushings every 6,000 miles (9,000 kilometers). Refer to **Figure 43** for the following procedure:

1. Remove hex nut, washer, and dust seal cap.

2. Slide pivot bolt out of center collar.

3. Remove center collar; grease inside of the pivot bushing; inside and outside of center collar; and outside of pivot bolt.

4. Assemble by reversing the preceding steps.

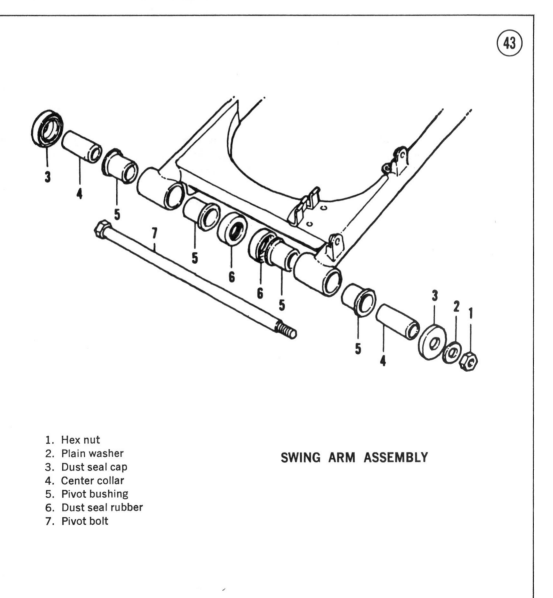

1. Hex nut
2. Plain washer
3. Dust seal cap
4. Center collar
5. Pivot bushing
6. Dust seal rubber
7. Pivot bolt

SWING ARM ASSEMBLY

CHAPTER THREE

TROUBLESHOOTING

Diagnosing motorcycle ills is relatively simple if you use orderly procedures and keep a few basic principles in mind.

Never assume anything. Don't overlook the obvious. If you are riding along and the bike suddenly quits, check the easiest, most accesible problem spots first. Is there gasoline in the tank? Is the gas petcock in the ON or RESERVE position? Has a spark plug wire fallen off? Check the ignition switch. Sometimes the weight of keys on a key ring may turn the ignition off suddenly.

If nothing obvious turns up in a cursory check, look a little further. Learning to recognize and describe symptoms will make repairs easier for you or a mechanic at the shop. Describe problems accurately and fully. Saying that "it won't run" isn't the same as saying "it quit on the highway at high speed and wouldn't start," or that "it sat in my garage for three months and then wouldn't start."

Gather as many symptoms together as possible to aid in diagnosis. Note whether the engine lost power gradually or all at once, what color smoke (if any) came from the exhausts, and so on. Remember that the more complicated a machine is, the easier it is to troubleshoot because symptoms point to specific problems.

You don't need fancy equipment or complicated test gear to determine whether repairs can be attempted at home. A few simple checks could save a large repair bill and time lost while the bike sits in a dealer's service department. On the other hand, be realistic and don't attempt repairs beyond your abilities. Service departments tend to charge heavily for putting together a disassembled engine that may have been abused. Some places won't even take on such a job — so use common sense and don't get in over your head.

OPERATING REQUIREMENTS

An engine needs three basics to run properly: correct gas-air mixture, compression, and a spark at the right time. If one or more are missing the engine won't run. The electrical system is the weakest link of the three. More problems result from electrical breakdowns than from any other source. Keep that in mind before you begin tampering with carburetor adjustments and the like.

If a bike has been sitting for any length of time and refuses to start, check the battery for a charged condition first and then look to the gasoline delivery system. This includes the tank, fuel petcocks, lines and the carburetor. Rust may have formed in the tank, obstructing fuel flow. Gasoline deposits may have gummed up carburetor jets and air passages. Gasoline tends to lose its potency after standing for long periods. Condensation may contaminate it with water. Drain old gas and try starting with a fresh tankful. Drain carburetor bowls too.

Compression, or the lack of it, usually enters the picture only in the case of older machines. Worn or broken pistons, rings, and cylinder bores could prevent starting. Generally, a gradual power loss and harder and harder starting will be readily apparent in this case.

STARTING DIFFICULTIES

Check gas flow first. Remove the gas cap and look into the tank. If gas is present, pull off a fuel line at the carburetor and see if gas flows freely. If none comes out, the fuel tap may be shut off, blocked by rust or foreign matter, or the fuel line may be stopped up or kinked. If the carburetor is getting usable fuel, turn to the electrical system next.

Check that the battery is charged by turning on the lights or by blowing the horn. Refer to your owner's manual for starting procedures with a dead battery. Have the battery recharged if necessary.

Pull off a spark plug cap, remove the spark plug and reconnect the cap. Lay the plug against the cylinder head so its base makes a good connection and turn the engine over with the kickstarter. A fat, blue spark should jump across the electrodes. If there is no spark, or a weak one, there is electrical system trouble. Check for a defective plug by replacing it with a known good one. Don't assume that a plug is good just because it's new.

Once the plug has been cleared of guilt, but there's still no spark, start backtracking through the system. If the contact at the end of the spark plug wire can be exposed it can be held about ⅛ inch from the head while the engine is turned over to check for a spark. Remember to hold the wire only by its insulation to avoid a nasty shock. If the plug wires are dirty, greasy, or wet, wrap a rag around them so you won't get shocked. If you do feel a shock or see sparks along the wire, clean or replace the wire and/or its connections.

If there's no spark at the plug wire, look for loose connections at the coil and battery. If all seems in order there, check next for oily or dirty

contact points. Clean points with electrical contact cleaner or a strip of paper. On battery ignition models, with the ignition switch turned on, open and close the points manually with a screwdriver.

No spark at the points with this test indicates a failure in the ignition system. Refer to *Ignition System Problems,* this chapter, for checkout procedures.

Refer to Chapter Two, *Ignition Timing* section for checking and setting ignition timing.

Note that spark plugs of the incorrect heat range (too cold) may cause hard starting. Set gaps to specifications. If you have just ridden through a puddle or washed the bike and it won't start, dry off plugs and plug wires. Water may have entered the carburetor and fouled the fuel under these conditions, but wet plugs and wires are the more likely problem.

If a healthy spark occurs at the right time, and there is adequate gas flow to the carburetor, check the carburetor itself at this time. Make sure all jets and air passages are clean, check float level and adjust if necessary. Shake the float to check for gasoline inside it and replace or repair as indicated. Check that the carburetors are mounted snugly and no air is leaking past the manifolds. Check for a clogged air filter.

Compression may be checked in the field by turning the kickstarter by hand and noting that adequate resistance is felt, or by removing a spark plug and placing a finger over the plug hole and feeling for pressure. Refer to Chapter Two for details on performing an engine compression test.

POOR IDLING

Poor idling may be caused by incorrect carburetor adjustment, incorrect timing, or ignition system defects. Check the gas cap vent for an obstruction.

MISFIRING

Misfirings can be caused by a weak spark or dirty plugs. Check for fuel contamination. Run the machine at night or in a darkened garage to check for spark leaks along the plug wires and under the spark plug cap. If misfiring occurs only at certain throttle settings, refer to the carburetor chapter for the specific carburetor circuits involved. Misfiring under heavy load, as when climbing hills or accelerating, is usually caused by bad spark plugs.

FLAT SPOTS

Poor condition of rings, pistons, or cylinders will cause a lack of power and speed. Ignition timing should be checked.

OVERHEATING

If the engine seems to run too hot all the time, be sure you are not idling it for long periods. Air cooled engines are not designed to operate at a standstill for any length of time. Heavy stop and go traffic is hard on a motorcycle engine. Spark plugs of the wrong heat range can burn pistons. An excessively lean gas mixture may cause overheating. Check ignition timing. Don't ride in too high a gear. Broken or worn rings and valves may permit compression gases to leak past them, heating heads and cylinders excessively. Check oil level and use the proper grade lubricants.

BACKFIRING

Check that timing is not advanced too far. Check fuel for contamination.

ENGINE NOISES

Experience is needed to diagnose accurately in this area. Noises are hard to differentiate and harder yet to describe. Deep knocking noises usually mean main bearing failure. A slapping noise generally comes from loose pistons. A light knocking noise during acceleration may be a bad connecting rod bearing. Pinging, which sounds like marbles being shaken in a tin can, is caused by ignition advanced too far or gasoline with too low an octane rating. Pinging should be corrected immediately or damage to pistons will result. Compression leaks at the head-cylinder joint will sound like a rapid on and off squeal.

PISTON SEIZURE

Piston seizure is caused by incorrect piston clearances when fitted, fitting rings with im-

proper end gap, too thin an oil being used, incorrect spark plug heat range, or incorrect ignition timing. Overheating from any cause may result in seizure.

EXCESSIVE VIBRATION

Excessive vibration may be caused by loose motor mounts, worn engine or transmission bearings, loose wheels, worn swinging arm bushings, a generally poor running engine, broken or cracked frame, or one that has been damaged in a collision. See also *Poor Handling*.

CLUTCH SLIP OR DRAG

Clutch slip may be due to worn plates, improper adjustment, or glazed plates. A dragging clutch could result from damaged or bent plates, improper adjustment, or even clutch spring pressure.

POOR HANDLING

Poor handling may be caused by improper tire pressures, a damaged frame or swinging arm, worn shocks or front forks, weak fork springs, a bent or broken steering stem, misaligned wheels, loose or missing spokes, worn tires, bent handlebars, worn wheel bearings or dragging brakes.

BRAKE PROBLEMS

Sticking brakes may be caused by broken or weak return springs, improper cable or rod adjustment, or dry pivot and cam bushings. Grabbing brakes may be caused by greasy linings which must be replaced. Brake grab may also be due to out-of-round drums or linings which have broken loose from the brake shoes. Glazed linings or glazed brake pads will cause loss of stopping power.

IGNITION SYSTEM PROBLEMS

Honda twin-cylinder models are equipped with a battery and coil ignition system, similiar in many ways to that of a conventional automobile.

Figure 1 illustrates a typical battery ignition

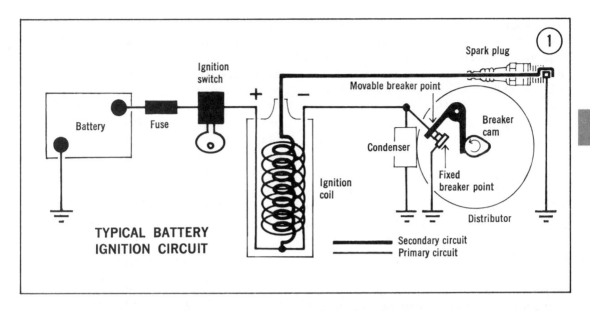

TYPICAL BATTERY
IGNITION CIRCUIT

Table 1   IGNITION SYSTEM PROBLEMS

Symptom	Probable Cause	Remedy
No spark or weak spark	Discharged battery	Charge battery
	Defective fuse	Replace
	Defective main switch	Replace
	Loose or corroded connections	Clean and tighten
	Broken wire	Repair
	Incorrect point gap	Reset points. Be sure to readjust ignition timing
	Dirty or oily points	Clean points
	Spark plug lead damaged	Replace wire
	Broken primary wire	Repair wire
	Open winding in coil	Replace coil
	Shorted winding in coil	Replace coil
	Defective condenser	Replace condenser

system for a single cylinder. Refer to that illustration during the following discussion.

Ignition system problems can be classified as no spark, weak spark, or improperly timed spark. **Table 1** lists common causes and remedies for ignition system malfunctions.

Disconnect the condenser and the wire from the points. Connect the ungrounded (positive) voltmeter lead to the wire which was connected to the points. If the voltmeter does not indicate battery voltage, the problem is an open coil primary circuit. Replace the suspected coil with a known good one. If the coil doesn't work, the problem is in the primary winding.

If the voltmeter indicates battery voltage, the coil primary circuit is OK. Connect the positive voltmeter lead to the wire which goes from the coil to the points. Block the points open with a business card or similar piece of cardboard. Connect the negative voltmeter lead to the movable point. If the voltmeter indicates any voltage, the points are shorted and must be replace.

If the foregoing checks are satisfactory, the problem is in the coil or condenser. Substitute each of these separately with a known good one to determine which is defective.

Ignition Coil

The ignition coil (**Figure 2**) is a form of transformer which develops the high voltage required to jump the spark plug gap. The only maintenance required is that of keeping the electrical connections clean and tight, and occasionally checking to see that the coil is mounted securely.

If the condition of the coil is doubtful, there are several checks which should be made.

1. Measure resistance between each primary terminal. Resistance should be about 2 to 5 ohms.

2. Measure resistance between each secondary wire. Resistance should be about 15,000 ohms.

3. Set the meter on the highest ohmmeter range. Determine that there is no continuity between either primary terminal and either secondary terminal.

4. Set the meter on the highest ohmmeter range. Determine that there is no continuity between either secondary terminal and the coil mounting bracket.

Condenser

The condenser is a sealed unit that requires no maintenance. Be sure that both connections are clean and tight.

Two tests can be made on the condenser. Measure condenser capacity with a condenser tester. Capacity should be about 0.2-0.3 microfarad. The other test is insulation resistance, which should not be less than 5 megohms, measured between the condenser pigtail and case.

In the event that no test equipment is available, a quick test of the condenser may be made by connecting the condenser case to the negative terminal of the motorcycle battery, and the positive lead to the positive battery terminal. Allow the condenser to charge for a few seconds, then quickly disconnect the battery and touch the condenser pigtail to the condenser case. If you observe a spark as the pigtail touches the case, you may assume that the condenser is OK.

Arching between the breaker points is a common symptom of condenser failure.

CHARGING SYSTEM

The charging system (**Figure 3**) on all Honda twins covered by this manual consists of an alternator, battery, and interconnecting wiring. Some models are also equipped with a solid state voltage regulator.

Alternator

An alternator (**Figure 4**) is a form of electrical generator in which a magnetized field rotor revolves within a set of stationary coils called a stator. As the rotor revolves, alternating current is induced in the stator. Stator current is then rectified and used to operate electrical accessories on the motorcycle and for battery charging.

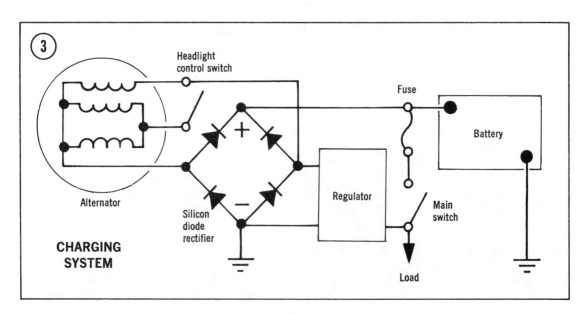

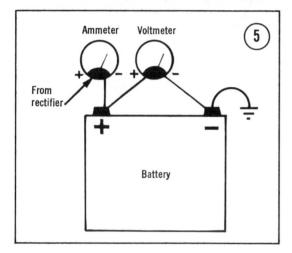

If alternator or regulator problems are suspected, as in the case of a chronically undercharged battery or dim headlights, first check the battery (refer to *Battery Service*). It must be

in good condition and at least half charged (1.220 specific gravity) before meaningful interpretation of test results can be made.

Connect 0-15 DC voltmeter and 0-10 DC ammeter as shown in **Figure 5**. Connect the positive ammeter terminal to the battery charging wire from the rectifier, and the negative ammeter terminal to the positive battery terminal. Connect the voltmeter positive lead to the battery charging lead and the negative terminal to a good ground.

> CAUTION
> *If the ammeter is connected between the battery positive terminal and the starter cable, do not attempt to start the engine with the electric starter. Starter current will burn out the ammeter.*

Start the engine and run it at the speeds listed in **Table 2**. Observe the voltmeter and ammeter and compare their indications with the specification. All measurements are made with lights on.

If charging current was considerably lower than specified, check the alternator and rectifier. Less likely is that charging current was too high; in that case, the regulator is probably at fault.

To check the alternator, proceed as follows.

1. Remove the alternator stator, then check for continuity between each pair of leads coming from it. If resistance between any pair of leads

Table 2 ALTERNATOR OUTPUT

Model	Charging Starts	Test Rpm	Minimum Voltage	Current (Amperes)
125/175 ①	1,900	5,000	7.0	1.7 minimum
		10,000	8.3	4.0 maximum
125	2,000	5,000	13.0	0.5 minimum
		10,000	16.5	3.0 maximum
160	2,000	5,000	13.0	0.5 minimum
		10,000	16.5	3.0 maximum
175	2,000	5,000	13.0	0.5 minimum
		10,000	16.5	3.0 maximum
200	2,000	5,000	14.0	0.5 minimum
		10,000	16.5	3.0 maximum
① 6-volt system				

differs greatly from that specified in **Table 3**, replace the stator.

2. Set the ohmmeter to its highest range, then check that there is no continuity between any lead and the stator frame. Replace the stator if there is any shorted lead.

3. Check all coils and wiring for chafing, broken connections, etc. Repair or replace as required.

4. Alternator rotors occasionally lose magnetism as a result of old age, presence of strong magnetic fields, or a sharp blow. Should the situation occur, it must be replaced.

Rectifier

All models are equipped with full-wave bridge rectifiers (refer to **Figure 6**). Checking procedures are similar for all; but the rectifiers differ in lead colors and connectors.

Some rectifiers mount by one terminal. The other terminals are leads, colored yellow, brown, and red/white. To test this rectifier, disconnect it from the motorcycle, then using an ohmmeter, measure resistance in both directions between the following pairs of terminals.

 a. Yellow and ground
 b. Brown and ground
 c. Yellow and red/white
 d. Brown and red/white

The second type rectifier has 4 leads, colored green, yellow, red/white or brown/white, and pink. To test this rectifier, measure resistance between each pair of wires listed:

 a. Green and yellow
 b. Green and pink
 c. Yellow and red/white or brown/white
 d. Pink and red/white or brown/white

On any type rectifier, resistance between each pair should be very high in one direction and low in the other. If resistance is either very high or very low in either direction, replace the rectifier assembly.

Always handle the rectifier assembly carefully. Do not bend or try to rotate the wafers. Do not loosen the screw which holds the assembly together. Moisture can damage the assembly, so keep it dry.

Table 3   TEST POINTS/RESISTANCE

Test Points	Resistance
Yellow - pink	1.1 ohm
Yellow/white - pink or white	0.5 ohm

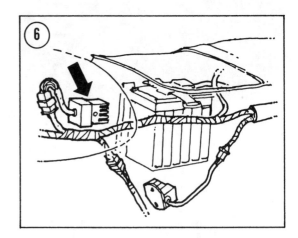

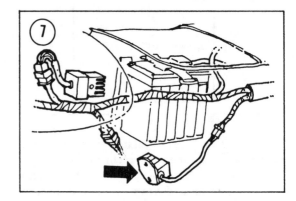

Never run the engine with the battery disconnected or without a fuse; doing so can cause immediate rectifier destruction.

Voltage Regulator

Problems with the voltage regulator (**Figure 7**) are rare. The simplest way to test it is to connect the test circuit shown in **Figure 5**, and compare battery charging current at various engine speeds with the regulator connected and disconnected. If charging current is limited to those values specified in **Table 2** when the regulator is connected, it is in good condition.

CAUTION
Do not disconnect or connect the regulator with the engine running.

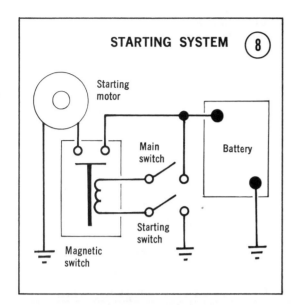

STARTING SYSTEM ⑧

Starting motor

Main switch

Battery

Starting switch

Magnetic switch

⑨

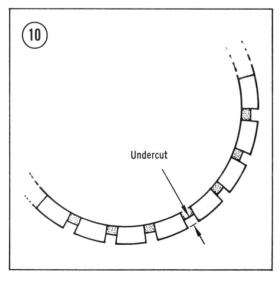

⑩

Undercut

ELECTRIC STARTER PROBLEMS

Figure 8 is a diagram of a typical starting system, showing the location of each component.

Circuit Operation

When the rider presses starter pushbutton, current flows from battery through the coil of starter relay if main switch is closed. Current through the relay coil causes its plunger to be pulled upward, thereby bridging the 2 heavy contacts in the starter relay, and completing the circuit from the battery to the starter motor.

Starter Motor

The starter motor (**Figure 9**) is wound in series for high torque, and draws approximately 120 amperes under normal starting conditions. This figure can vary considerably, depending on engine temperature, starter condition, and other factors.

If starter problems are encountered, overhaul is best performed by a shop specializing in small motor repair or auto electrical systems. Some checks and service can be done by the layman, however.

1. Remove and disassemble the starter motor.

2. If either brush is excessively worn, replace both brushes.

3. Examine the commutator for roughness or burning. Minor roughness may be smoothed with fine sandpaper. After smoothing, be sure that the mica insulators between commutator segments are undercut to a depth of at least 0.012 inch (0.3 millimeter), as shown in **Figure 10**.

4. Use an armature growler or ohmmeter to determine that no commutator segment is shorted to the shaft.

5. Using an ohmmeter, determine that there is continuity between every adjacent pair of commutator segments.

6. With the starter disassembled, determine that there is continuity between the ungrounded brush holder and the starter terminal.

7. Using the highest ohmmeter range, determine that there is no continuity between the

Table 4   STARTER TROUBLESHOOTING

Symptom	Probable Cause	Remedy
Starter does not work	Low battery	Recharge battery
	Worn brushes	Replace brushes
	Internal short	Repair or replace defective component
	Defective wiring or connections	Repair wire or clean and tighten connections
	Defective switch	Replace switch
Starter action is weak	Low battery	Recharge battery
	Pitted relay contacts	Clean contacts or replace voltage regulator
	Brushes worn	Replace brushes
	Defective wiring or connections	Repair wire or clean and tighten
	Short in armature	Replace armature
Starter runs continuously	Stuck relay	Dress contacts
Starter turns but engine does not	Defective starter drive	Repair or replace starter drive

starter terminal and starter motor housing.

Table 4 lists symptoms, probable causes, and remedies for possible starter malfunctions.

Starter Drive

The starter turns the engine through a chain and overrunning clutch (**Figure 11**).

To check the starter drive, it is only necessary to check that it transmits torque in one direction only. Disassemble the unit and check all springs and rollers in the event of malfuntion.

Starter Relay

After long service, contacts in the starter relay may pit and burn, or the coil may burn out. To test this unit, connect the motorycycle battery between the relay coil terminals (usually yellow/red and black). If no click occurs, replace the relay. If the relay clicks, the relay coil is OK, but its contacts may be pitted or burned. To correct this problem, disassemble the starter relay and lightly dress its contacts with a fine file. Don't remove any more metal than necessary.

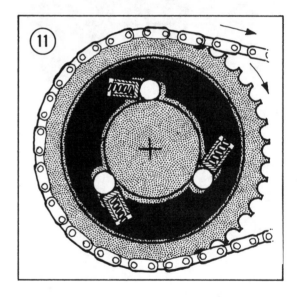

LIGHTING PROBLEMS

The headlight assembly consists primarily of a headlight lens and reflector unit, and related hardware.

In the event of lighting troubles, first check the affected bulb. Poor ground connections are another cause of lamp malfunctions.

Turn signals usually operate from direct current supplied by the battery. When replacing the signal bulbs, always be sure to use the proper type. Erratic operation or even failure to flash may result from use of wrong bulbs.

Stoplights usually operate from direct current also. Stoplight switches should be adjusted so that the lamp comes on just before braking action begins. Front brake stoplight switches are frequently built into the front brake cable, and are not adjustable.

Bulbs which continuously burn out may be caused by excessive vibration, loose connections that permit sudden current surges, poor battery connections, or installation of the wrong type bulb.

A dead battery, or one which discharges quickly, may be caused by a faulty generator or rectifier. Check for loose or corroded terminals.

Shorted battery cells or broken terminals will keep a battery from charging. Low water level will decrease a battery's capacity. A battery left uncharged after installation will sulphate, rendering it useless. Refer to Chapter Two, *Battery Service* section.

A majority of light and horn or other electrical accessory problems are caused by loose or corroded ground connections. Check those first and then substitute known good units for easier troubleshooting.

HORN PROBLEMS

A typical horn circuit is shown in **Figure 12**. Current for the horn is supplied by the battery. One terminal is connected to the battery through the main switch . The other terminal is grounded when the horn button is pressed.

The horn (**Figure 13**) will not sound if its contact points are burned. Dress them with a small point file of flex stone. Adjust horn tone after dressing the contact points (refer to Chapter Six, *Horn* section).

3

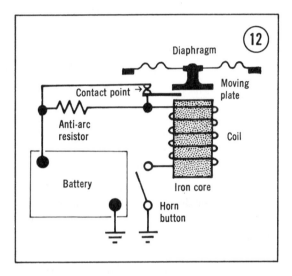

CHAPTER FOUR

ENGINE, TRANSMISSION, AND CLUTCH

This chapter describes removal, disassembly, service, and reassembly of the engine, transmission, and clutch. Engine removal is not necessary for service operations on alternators, oil pump, clutches, or the shifter mechanism.

SERVICE HINTS

Experience has shown that work goes faster and easier if certain standard shop practices are observed. Some of the more important ones are listed below:

1. During engine disassembly, keep all related parts together. Reassembly will be much easier if this precaution is taken, in particular if a long period lapses between disassembly and reassembly.

2. All O-rings, gaskets, snap rings, and cotter pins which are removed should be replaced.

3. Be sure all parts are clean upon reassembly.

4. Lubricate all moving parts liberally before reassembly.

5. On parts attached with multiple bolts or screws, tighten those of larger diameter first. If parts are attached with inner and outer bolts or screws, tighten inner ones first.

ENGINE REMOVAL

Engine removal is generally similar for all models listed in this manual. The following steps are set forth as a guide.

1. Warm the engine if possible, then drain engine oil into a pan.

2. Turn fuel petcock selector lever to STOP, then remove fuel lines from fuel petcock (**Figure 1**).

3. Remove battery cable (**Figure 2**).

4. Remove gas tank (**Figure 3**).

5. Remove carburetors from cylinder head (leave carburetors attached to the air filter intakes). See **Figure 4**.

6. Remove exhaust pipe-to-cylinder head nuts (**Figure 5**).

7. Disconnect spark plug leads and disconnect from clips (**Figure 6**).

8. Remove rear muffler bracket (**Figure 7**) and exhaust pipe bracket above left footpeg (**Figure 8**).

9. Remove entire exhaust system (pull the collars out of the cylinder head and dismantle all brackets).

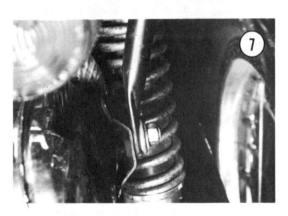

10. Remove footpegs to aid in engine removal (**Figure 9**).

11. Disconnect breaker point wire (**Figure 10**).

12. Remove the countershaft sprocket cover (**Figure 11**).

13. Disconnect clutch cable (**Figure 12**).

14. Remove countershaft sprocket (put bike in gear in order to aid in nut removal) and let chain dangle (**Figure 13**).

15. Loosen alternator wiring (**Figure 14**).

16. Remove tachometer drive cover (**Figure 15**) and remove screw that holds tachometer cable. Pull cable out, then reinstall screw (**Figure 16**).

17. Cut the tie-wrap holding the alternator plug and disconnect the plug (**Figure 17**).

18. Pull off the breather tube from the cylinder head (**Figure 18**).

19. Push boot covering starter cable connection back and disconnect starter cable connection (**Figure 19**). Pry the clip holding the cable under the starter to one side (**Figure 20**) and let the cable dangle. (There is also a clip behind the shift lever; free the cable at this point also.)

20. Remove the wire connecting the condenser to the coil (**Figure 21**).

21. Remove the cylinder head bracket bolts and remove bracket completely (**Figure 22**).

22. Remove the front engine mounting bolts (**Figure 23**).

23. Remove rear engine mounting bolts, then lift engine slightly and slide both rear mounting bolts out (**Figure 24**).

24. Lift engine out of the left side of the frame.

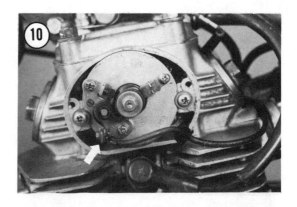

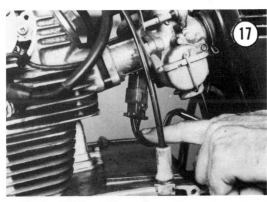

4

PRELIMINARY ENGINE DISMANTLING

Work on the engine will progress faster if you remove all parts necessary on the left side of the engine first, then on the right (this is assuming that a complete engine overhaul is necessary).

Left Side of Engine

1. Remove shift lever (**Figure 25**).
2. Remove alternator cover screws (**Figure 26**)

4

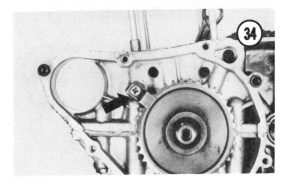

and tap cover off with a rubber mallet (**Figure 27**).

3. Remove clip holding alternator main wiring harness (**Figure 28**).

4. Remove neutral indicator switch (**Figure 29**).

5. Remove starter motor retaining screws (**Figure 30**) and tap starter motor out of case (rearward) with a rubber mallet (**Figure 31**).

6. Remove chain and sprocket (**Figure 32**).

7. Remove alternator retaining nut and pull alternator with a suitable puller (**Figure 33**).

8. Remove starter sprocket setting plate (**Figure 34**), then remove starter sprocket.

Right Side of Engine

1. Remove kickstarter lever (**Figure 35**).

2. Remove crankcase cover (**Figure 36**).

3. Remove kickstarter spring (**Figure 37**).

4. Remove the screw holding oil filter cap (**Figure 38**).

5. Remove 6mm center screw, then screw in a 8mm bolt as an extractor and pull on screw with a pair of pliers (**Figure 39**).

6. Remove the slotted nut that holds on the oil filter with a special tool available at your dealer (**Figure 40**).

CLUTCH AND OIL PUMP

On all models, the clutch is located under the right crankcase cover, and may be serviced without engine removal.

The oil pump is driven by an eccentric cam on the engine side of the clutch housing which drives a pushrod to operate the oil pump plunger.

Removal

1. Remove hex bolts that hold clutch springs (**Figure 41**).

> NOTE: *Loosen each hex nut a little bit at a time to equalize pressure.*

2. Remove clutch springs (**Figure 42**), then remove clutch pressure plate (**Figure 43**).

3. Pull out the clutch friction discs and plates all at one time (**Figure 44**).

4. Remove the push crown, then remove the clutch hub snap ring (**Figure 45**).

5. Remove the clutch hub (**Figure 46**).

4

6. Remove the primary drive gear, then bend the locking tabs up on the oil pump and remove the bolts (**Figure 47**).

7. Remove the oil pump and clutch shell at the same time (**Figure 48**).

8. Remove remaining primary gear (**Figure 49**).

Inspection

1. Measure thickness of each friction disc with vernier calipers. Replace all discs if any disc is worn to its wear limit, as specified in **Table 1**.

2. Place each clutch plate on a flat surface. Using a feeler gauge, measure clutch plate warpage. Replace plates if any plate is warped more than 0.012 in. (0.3mm).

3. Measure free length of each clutch spring. Replace all springs as a set if any spring is shorter than its service limit, specified in **Table 2**.

Table 1   CLUTCH DISC SPECIFICATIONS

Model	Standard Thickness		Wear Limit	
	Inches	Millimeters	Inches	Millimeters
CA125	0.138	3.5	0.134	3.4
All other 125's and all 160 and 175 models	0.118	3.0	0.114	2.9
200	0.118	3.0	0.102	2.6

Table 2   CLUTCH SPRING SPECIFICATIONS

Model	Standard Length		Service Limit	
	Inches	Millimeters	Inches	Millimeters
125,160	(not specified)		(not specified)	
175	1.40	35.5	1.35	34.2
200	1.15	28.3	1.05	26.7

Installation

1. Install primary gear (refer to **Figure 49**).

2. Install oil pump and clutch shell as a unit (refer to **Figure 48**).

3. Install the primary drive gear, then install the oil pump retaining bolts. Fold the locking tabs over securely (refer to **Figure 47**).

4. Install the clutch hub (refer to **Figure 46**).

5. Install the clutch hub snap ring and install the push crown (refer to **Figure 45**).

6. Insert clutch friction discs and plates (refer to **Figure 44**).

> NOTE: *The dished steel plate goes in first, then a friction disc, steel disc, friction disc, etc.*

7. Insert each clutch spring (refer to **Figure 42**), then install the clutch pressure plate (refer to **Figure 43**).

8. Tighten each hex bolt that holds the clutch springs a little bit at a time to avoid distortion (refer to **Figure 41**). Tighten hex bolts securely.

SHIFTER MECHANISM

Removal

1. Loosen nut on gearshift stopper plate and remove outer stopper (**Figure 50**).

2. On left side of engine, remove snap ring that holds the gearshift shaft (**Figure 51**).

3. Tap the gearshift shaft out of the right side of the engine (**Figure 52**).

> NOTE: *Do not lose the flat washer on left side of engine (it is located under the snap ring).*

4. On right side of engine, remove spacer and shift cam inner stopper (**Figure 53**).

Installation

1. Install spacer and shift cam inner stopper on right side of engine (refer to **Figure 53**).

2. Tap the gearshift shaft into the right side of the engine (refer to **Figure 52**).

3. On the left side of the engine, position the flat washer that sits under the snap ring, then

install the snap ring that holds the gearshift shaft on (refer to **Figure 51**).

4. Install the outer stopper, then install nut on gearshift stopper plate (refer to **Figure 50**).

CYLINDER HEAD

Cylinder Head Removal

1. Remove tappet adjustment covers (**Figure 54**), then loosen tappet adjusting locknuts and tappet adjusting screws.

2. Remove cylinder head cover (eight, 8mm nuts and one, 6mm bolt). Make a note of where the condenser connects to the cylinder head so you can reinstall it in the correct position (**Figure 55**).

3. Remove breaker point cover (**Figure 56**).

4. Remove breaker point base plate after removing its retaining screw (**Figure 57**).

5. Remove the 5mm bolt and slide the spark advance mechanism out (**Figure 58**).

6. Turn engine over until pistons are at TDC (the alternator should be on the T mark (**Figure 59**); the camshaft sprocket should have the O facing up (**Figure 60**); and the pin which locates the auto advance unit should face up (**Figure 61**).

7. Loosen the cam chain tensioner adjusting bolt (**Figure 62**), then remove all tension from the chain.

8. Remove master link in cam chain.

> NOTE: *Stuff a clean shop cloth under the master link before disconnecting the chain, to avoid losing the link down in the engine.*

9. Tie a piece of wire to each end of the cam chain and wrap it around any external engine component to keep from losing the chain down inside the engine (**Figure 63**).

10. Remove the cylinder head and old gasket (tap on the cylinder head with a rubber mallet to loosen it).

> ### CAUTION
> *Be careful that you do not lose the locating dowels. Discard the old O-rings and replace with new ones or oil leakage will occur* (**Figure 64**).

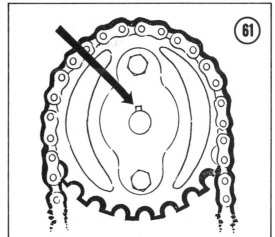

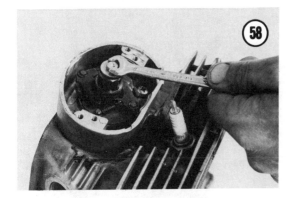

Inspection

1. Refer to **Figure 65**. Measure the cylinder head warpage with a straightedge and feeler gauge. Warpage must not exceed 0.002 in. (0.05mm). If clearance exceeds that value, re-surface or replace the cylinder head.

2. Remove carbon from each combustion chamber with a wire brush chucked into an electric drill. (This operation is easier with valves still installed in the cylinder head.)

Valve Service

Valve service is best left to a machine shop which has the experience and equipment to handle small engines. Service procedures are given for those of you with the proper equipment to handle this operation.

1. Compress each valve spring and remove the valve keeper (**Figure 66**).

2. Remove the valve spring compressor, then the valve springs and valve components (refer to **Figure 67**, left to right: valve spring seat; outer spring; inner spring; top collar; valve; O-seal; and split collar).

3. Measure side clearance of each valve while it is positioned in the cylinder head, using a dial indicator. Refer to **Table 3** and replace any valve and/or its guide if clearance exceeds the service limits specified.

4. Measure valve stem diameter at 3 locations on the valve stem. Refer to **Table 4**. Replace any valve if its stem is worn to less than the service limits specified.

> NOTE: *When replacing valves, it is recommended that valve guides be replaced also. To do so, tap the guide from the cylinder head with a valve driving tool and a light hammer. Always install oversize guides when replacement is necessary, and then ream to fit. Valve guide tools and reamers may be obtained through your Honda dealer.*

5. Measure width of each valve face as shown in **Figure 68**. Refer to **Table 5**. Grind valves to service limits specified.

6. Measure free length of each valve spring as shown in **Figure 69**. Refer to **Table 6**. Replace

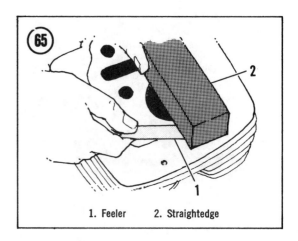

1. Feeler   2. Straightedge

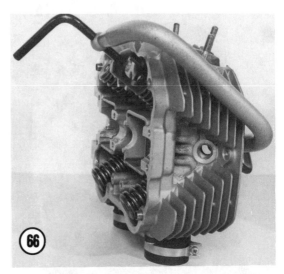

Table 3   VALVE STEM CLEARANCE

Model	Service Limit	
	Inches	Millimeters
125, 160, 175, 200		
Intake	0.0032	0.08
Exhaust	0.0039	0.10

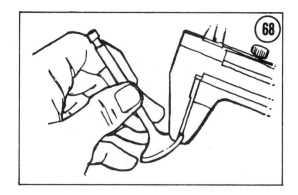

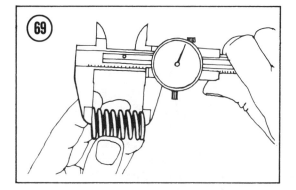

Table 4   VALVE STEM SERVICE LIMITS

| Model | Service Limit | |
	Inches	Millimeters
125, 160, 175		
Intake	0.2134	5.42
Exhaust	0.2126	5.40
200		
Intake	0.0032	5.42
Exhaust	0.2126	5.40

Table 6   VALVE SPRING FREE LENGTH

Model	Inches	Millimeters
CB125, CB160		
Outer	1.38	35.0
Inner	1.04	26.3
CD125, all 175		
Outer	1.20	30.6
Inner	1.10	27.9
200		
Outer	1.36	34.5
Inner	1.26	32.0

any valve spring with a free length shorter than that specified in the service limits.

7. Install the valve seat (**Figure 70**). Then install the seal, springs, and top collar. Compress the springs with a valve spring compressor and install the keeper (**Figure 71**).

Camshaft Removal/Installation

1. Remove the cylinder head side covers (**Figure 72**).

Table 5   VALVE FACE WIDTH

| Model | Standard Width | | Service Limit | |
	Inches	Millimeters	Inches	Millimeters
125, 160, 175	0.028-0.039	0.7-1.0	0.071	1.8
200	0.039-0.055	1.0-1.4	0.071	1.8

2. Remove tachometer gear (**Figure 73**).

3. Remove rocker arm shafts and rocker arms (**Figure 74**).

4. The hollow dowel in the end of the camshaft must be removed in order to get the camshaft out of the head (refer to **Figure 73**). To avoid distorting the dowel during removal, insert the end of a rocker arm shaft into the end of the hollow dowel and pull dowel out of the head with a pair of pliers.

5. Remove the camshaft and clean the head thoroughly in solvent and hot water (**Figure 75**).

6. To install the camshaft, proceed as follows:

   a. Lay the camshaft in the head (**Figure 76**).

   b. Drop a 8mm bolt into the hole as shown in **Figure 77**. This keeps the rocker arm shaft from being inserted too far. Position the rocker arms and insert the rocker arm shaft (**Figure 78**).

   c. Remove the 8mm bolt used in Step 6b, preceding.

   d. Coat one side cover with gasket sealer and set the gasket in place (**Figure 79**).

   e. Position the side cover and install the bolts (**Figure 80**).

   f. Install both rocker arms at opposite end of cylinder head as you did in Step 6b, preceding.

   g. Tap the hollow dowel into the end of the camshaft (**Figure 81**).

   h. Install the tachometer gear (**Figure 82**).

   i. Install the side cover on opposite end of camshaft (turn cam until tachometer gear engages).

Cylinder Head Installation

1. Clean old gasket material from cylinder head and cylinder mating surfaces, and install a new gasket (coat the cylinder base with gasket cement).

> CAUTION
> *Be careful that you do not lose the dowels. Be sure to discard the old O-rings and replace them with new ones, or oil leakage will be sure to occur (**Figure 83**).*

4

2. Install the cylinder head and pull the drive chain up through the opening in the cylinder head with the wires that are connected to each end of the chain (**Figure 84**).

3. Turn crankshaft over until pistons are at TDC. The alternator should be on the T mark (**Figure 85**). The camshaft sprocket should have the O facing up and the pin which locates the auto advance unit should face up (**Figure 86**).

4. Install the cam sprocket so that the alignment marks are parallel to the upper surface of the cylinder head (**Figure 87**). Install one sprocket mounting bolt, then turn crankshaft over (use a wrench on the alternator bolt) and install the remaining bolt. Turn the crankshaft over again so that all marks are as indicated in Step 3, preceding.

5. Stuff a clean shop cloth under the master link to avoid losing the link inside the engine (**Figure 88**). Install the master link exactly as indicated in **Figure 89**.

> NOTE: *A good precautionary check before connecting the master link is to hold the chain taut as illustrated in* **Figure 90** *and turn the alternator with a wrench to be sure that the chain is on the crankshaft sprocket.*

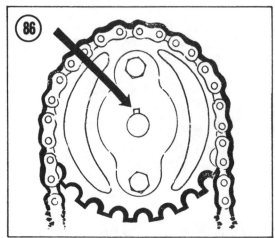

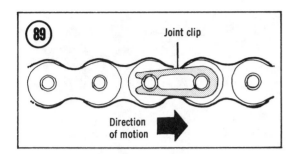

Joint clip

Direction of motion

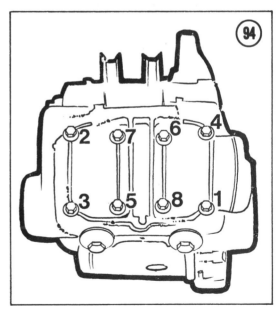

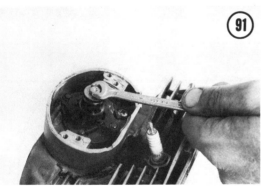

6. Install the spark advance mechanism with the 5mm bolt (**Figure 91**).

7. Install the breaker point base plate and tighten the retaining screw (**Figure 92**). Leave the breaker cover off for later breaker point adjustment procedure.

8. Install cylinder head cover (eight 8mm nuts, and one 6mm bolt). See **Figure 93**. Torque 125-175cc models to 11.6-15.2 ft.-lb. (160-210 mkg); 200cc models to 13-16 ft.-lb. (180-220 mkg) in the order shown in **Figure 94** (125-175cc models) or **Figure 95** (200cc models).

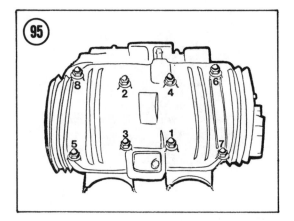

9. Adjust the cam chain tension by loosening the locknut on the cam chain tensioner (**Figure 96**), backing off on the adjusting screw, and tightening it up again. Secure with the locknut.

10. Adjust the valve timing as follows:

   a. Turn crankshaft over with a wrench on the alternator retaining nut until the breaker points are open to the maximum gap (**Figure 97**).

   b. Measure the breaker point gap with a feeler gauge (**Figure 98**). Point gap should be 0.012-0.016 in. (0.30-0.40mm). If so, go on to Step 10f. If adjustment is necessary, continue with Step 10c.

   c. Refer to **Figure 97**. Slightly loosen the base plate retaining screws.

   d. Move the base plate until the point gap is 0.014 in. (0.35mm) as shown in **Figure 97**.

   e. Tighten both base plate retaining screws, then check gap again. Readjust if necessary.

   f. Rotate the engine until the points are fully open on the remaining lobe of the contact breaker cam. Perform the preceding steps once more (this is to adjust the breaker point gap for the other cylinder).

   g. Wipe the breaker cam clean, then apply a very small quantity of breaker cam lubricant. Apply just enough to create an oil film on the cam; more may cause point failure.

   h. Place a wrench on the alternator retaining bolt and turn the engine over until the F

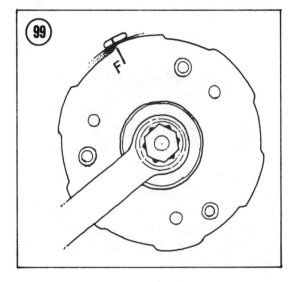

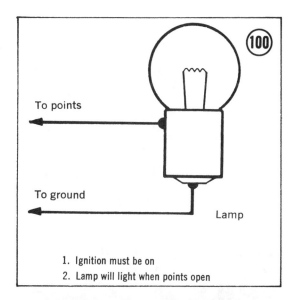

mark on the alternator rotor aligns with the index pointer (**Figure 99**).

i. Connect a timing tester to the breaker point terminal and a good ground (follow the manufacturer's hook-up instructions). If no timing tester is available, make up a test lamp as shown in **Figure 100**.

j. Loosen both base plate retaining screws (refer to **Figure 98**) just enough so that the base plate can be moved slightly. Turn the base plate gradually until the points just begin to open (if a test lamp is used to determine point opening, be sure that the ignition switch is ON). The test lamp will light exactly at the moment that the F mark on the alternator rotor aligns with the index pointer, if the ignition timing is correct (**Figure 101**).

k. Tighten the base plate retaining screws.

l. Recheck adjustment by turning the rotor clockwise slowly, then counterclockwise slowly. The F mark and index should align just as the points open (and the test lamp lights up). Readjust if necessary.

m. To check the remaining cylinder, turn the rotor one full revolution (360 degrees) and perform the preceding steps again.

11. Install breaker point cover (**Figure 102**).

12. Adjust the valve clearance as follows:

a. Turn engine over until the T mark on the alternator rotor aligns with its index pointer (refer to **Figure 103**).

b. Check both cylinders to see which one has both valves closed. Adjust the valves on that cylinder by loosening the locknut and turning the valve adjuster until the clearance between the valve stem and adjuster screw is 0.002 in. (0.05mm) for each valve (**Figure 104**). Tighten the locknut and recheck the adjustment; readjust if necessary.

c. Turn engine one complete revolution (360 degrees), then repeat preceding steps for remaining cylinder.

d. Install tappet covers (**Figure 105**) and alternator cover (**Figure 106**).

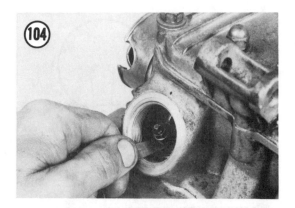

CYLINDERS AND PISTONS

The cylinders are of cast lightweight aluminum alloy, and have cast iron liners of sufficient thickness to permit boring and honing after long usage or a piston seizure. Pistons are of lightweight aluminum alloy.

Cylinder Removal

1. Remove the cylinder head (refer to *Cylinder Head, Removal*, preceding section).

2. Remove cylinder retaining bolt (**Figure 107**).

3. Tap the cylinders with a rubber mallet to loosen them. Pull cylinders off (**Figure 108**).

Checking Cylinders

Measure cylinder diameter at the top, middle, and bottom of each cylinder, using an accurate cylinder gauge. Measurements should be made both parallel and at a right angle to the crankshaft at each measurement depth. If any measurement exceeds the wear limit specified in **Table 7**, or if any 2 measurements differ by 0.002 in. (0.05mm), rebore and hone the cylinder to the next oversize. Pistons are available in oversizes of 0.25, 0.50, 0.75, and 1.00mm.

Table 7   CYLINDER WEAR LIMITS

Model	Inches	Millimeters
125	1.736	44.1
160	1.972	50.1
175	2.051	52.1
200	2.189	55.6

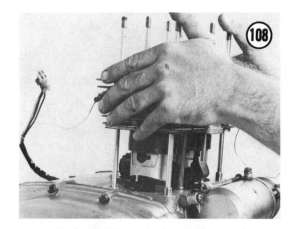

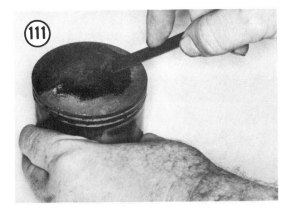

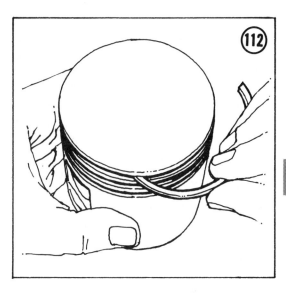

After boring and honing, the difference between maximum and minimum measurements should not exceed 0.002 in. (0.05mm).

Piston Removal

1. Support the pistons with a piece of wood and remove the outside piston pin clip (**Figure 109**).

2. Drive the piston pin out (**Figure 110**) and remove the piston.

> NOTE: *If piston pin is a very tight fit, lay rags soaked in hot water around the piston. The pin will come out quite easily after a few moments. Wipe up any excess hot water with a soft, clean cloth.*

Piston Ring Replacement

1. Spread the top piston ring with a thumb on each end of the ring, and remove it from top of the piston. Take care not to scratch the piston. Repeat this procedure for each remaining ring.

2. Scrape heavy carbon deposits from the piston head (**Figure 111**). A broken hacksaw blade with its corners slightly rounded makes a good scraper.

3. Clean carbon and gum from the piston ring grooves (**Figure 112**), using a broken piston ring. Any deposits remaining in ring grooves will cause replacement rings to stick, thereby causing gas blow-by and loss of power.

4. Measure piston rings for wear as shown in **Figure 113**. Insert each piston ring into the cylinder to a depth of 0.2 in. (5mm). To ensure that the ring is squarely in the cylinder, push it into position with the piston head. Standard gaps and wear limits are specified in **Table 8**. Replace all rings if any ring is worn so much that the piston ring gap exceeds the wear limit.

5. Before installing rings, check the fit of each one in its groove. To do so, slip the outer surface of the ring into its groove, then roll the ring completely around the piston (**Figure 114**). If any binding occurs, determine and correct its cause before proceeding.

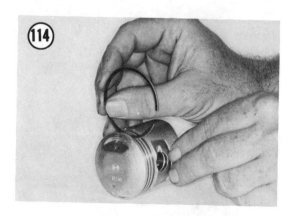

6. After installation, measure clearance between each ring and its groove at several places around the piston, as shown in **Figure 115**. Replace the ring and/or piston if ring groove clearance exceeds service limits specified in **Table 9**.

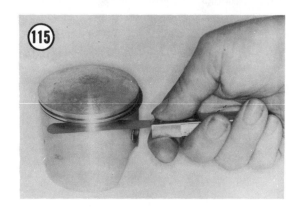

7. When replacing piston rings, install the lower one first. Be sure that they are installed so that all manufacturer's marks are toward the piston crown. If this precaution is not observed, oil pumping will occur. Position piston rings so that their gaps are staggered at 120-degree intervals (**Figure 116**).

Piston Clearance

Piston clearance is the difference between maximum piston diameter and minimum cylinder diameter. Measure piston diameter across the piston skirt (**Figure 117**) at right angles to the piston pin. Standard piston clearances and wear limits are listed in **Table 10**.

A piston showing signs of seizure will result in noise, loss of power, and cylinder wall dam-

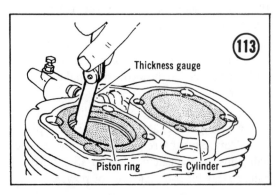

Thickness gauge

Piston ring   Cylinder

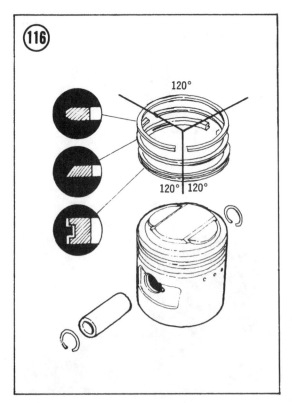

120°

120° 120°

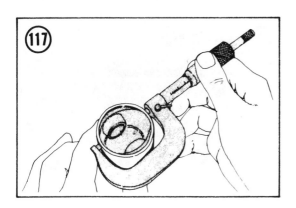

age. If such a piston is reused without correction, another seizure will develop. To correct this condition, lightly smooth the affected area with No. 400 emery paper or a fine oilstone. Replace any piston which is deeply scratched.

Piston Pins

Measure piston pin diameter at its center and at both ends. Also measure piston pin bore in the piston. Standard clearance should be 0.0001-0.0006 in. (0.002-0.014mm). Replace

Table 8   PISTON RING GAP

Model	Standard Value		Wear Limit	
	Inches	Millimeters	Inches	Millimeters
125, 160, 175	0.006	0.15	0.031	0.80
200	0.006	0.15	0.029	0.75

Table 9   PISTON RING GROOVE CLEARANCE

Model	Standard Clearance		Service Limit	
	Inches	Millimeters	Inches	Millimeters
CB125				
Compression	0.0006-0.0017	0.015-0.045	0.0236	0.60
Oil	0.0004-0.0017	0.010-0.045	0.0236	0.60
CD125				
Compression	0.0006-0.0017	0.015-0.045	0.0236	0.60
Oil	0.0006-0.0017	0.015-0.045	0.0236	0.60
160				
Compression	0.0006-0.0017	0.015-0.045	0.0236	0.60
Oil	0.0004-0.0017	0.010-0.045	0.0236	0.60
175				
Compression	0.0006-0.0017	0.015-0.045	0.0236	0.60
Oil	0.0006-0.0017	0.015-0.045	0.0236	0.60
200				
Compression	0.0016-0.0030	0.040-0.075	0.006	0.15
Second	0.0010-0.0024	0.025-0.060	0.006	0.15
Oil	0.0006-0.0018	0.015-0.045	0.006	0.15

Table 10   PISTON CLEARANCE

Model	Standard Clearance		Wear Limit	
	Inches	Millimeters	Inches	Millimeters
CB125	0.0004-0.0040	0.01-0.10	0.008	0.20
CD125	0.0004-0.0020	0.01-0.05	0.008	0.20
160	0.004-0.0080	0.10-0.20	0.010	0.25
175 and 200	0.0004-0.0020	0.01-0.05	0.008	0.20

the pistons and/or piston pin if clearance exceeds 0.0047 in. (0.12mm).

Piston Installation

1. Coat pistons with assembly oil and set in position over the connecting rods and insert the piston pins. (If pins go in hard, soak pistons in hot water; the pin will push in easily. Wipe excess water off with a soft, clean cloth.)

> NOTE: *If* IN *is stamped on the piston, that mark should be toward the intake valve at the rear. If an arrow is stamped on the piston, it should face the front of the engine.*

2. Install new piston pin clips (refer to **Figure 110**).

Cylinder Installation

1. Coat the cylinder bore with assembly oil.

2. Coat the cylinder base with gasket cement, then install a new gasket (**Figure 118**).

3. Set the cylinder carefully over the studs (**Figure 119**).

4. Gently depress the piston rings with a screwdriver (be careful not to nick the metal). See **Figure 120**.

5. Push the cylinder firmly down on the crankcase and install the cylinder retaining bolt (**Figure 121**).

> CAUTION
> *Be sure that the cylinder locating dowels are in position.*

CAM CHAIN TENSIONER

Engine valves and ignition breaker points are operated by a chain-driven camshaft. Slack develops in this chain, which can result in retarded ignition and valve timing, and a consequent loss of power. A cam chain tensioner automatically takes up slack in the cam chain.

No service is required on this unit other than to check for wear on the tensioner roller and guide roller.

Removal and Installation

1. Remove the cylinder head (refer to *Cylinder*

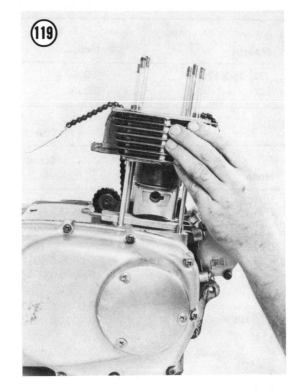

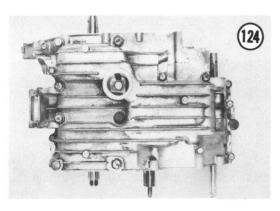

Head section, this chapter) and the cylinders (refer to *Cylinders and Pistons* section, this chapter).

2. Remove the retaining bolts shown in **Figure 122** and lift the cam chain tensioner out. Inspect for wear or damage.

3. Install by reversing the preceding steps.

Adjustment

Refer to **Figure 123** for the following steps.

1. Loosen locknut, then slightly loosen bolt. The cam chain slack will be taken up automatically by spring pressure.

2. Tighten bolt, then hold in place and tighten locknut.

CRANKCASE

Crankcases on all models split into upper and lower halves without special tools. It is necessary to split crankcase halves to service the crankshaft, transmission, internal shifter components, and kickstarter. Although details differ slightly between various models, the following service procedures are generally applicable to all models.

Disassembly

1. Remove the cylinder head, cylinder, and pistons, as outlined in previous sections.

2. Turn engine upside down and remove the nine 6mm crankcase bolts, and seven 8mm bolts (**Figure 124**).

> NOTE: *Make a note of where the starter cable connects so you can install it correctly during the reassembly sequence.*

3. Remove the drain plug and remove the bolt under the drain (refer to **Figure 124**).

4. Tap on the engine mounting boss with a rubber mallet to separate the cases.

Inspection

Lubricating oil passages are machined in the crankcase. Be very careful that these passages do not become clogged during service operations. If any passage is clogged, blow it out with compressed air. Examine mating surfaces of both halves for nicks or scratches which will result in oil leaks. Clean off all traces of old sealing compound.

Reassembly

1. Be sure that mating surfaces of both crankcase halves are clean.

2. Coat mating surfaces with liquid gasket compound.

> **CAUTION**
> *Do not get gasket compound on dowel pins or surfaces which do not mate.*

3. Assemble both crankcase halves and install bolts. Torque the 8mm bolts to 11.5-12.2 ft.-lb. (1.6-1.7 mkg); the 6mm bolts to 5.8-6.5 ft.-lb. (0.8-0.9 mkg).

CRANKSHAFT

The crankshaft operates under conditions of high stress. Dimensional tolerances are critical. It is necessary to locate and correct crankshaft defects early to prevent more serious troubles later.

Removal and Installation

1. Split the crankcase halves (refer to *Crankcase* section, preceding).

2. Lift out the crankshaft.

3. To install the crankshaft, reverse the preceding steps.

Inspection

Measurement locations and support points are shown in **Figure 125**. Replace the crankshaft if runout exceeds 0.118 in. (3.0mm) at locations C, D, E, or F. Maximum runout tolerance at locations A or B is 0.006 in. (0.15mm).

TRANSMISSION

Removal

1. Split the crankcase and remove the crankshaft as outlined in preceding sections.

2. Lift out the input shaft and the output shaft (**Figure 126**).

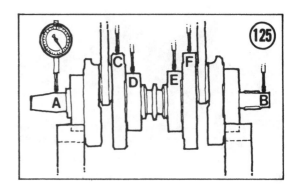

3. Remove the kickstarter shaft (refer to **Figure 126**).

Inspection

1. Measure backlash between each pair of gears. Replace gears in pairs if backlash exceeds 0.008 in. (0.2mm).

2. Check gear teeth for wear, nicks, or burrs. Minor defects may be smoothed with an oilstone. If one gear requires replacement, it is good practice to replace its mating gear also.

3. Be sure that sliding gears move smoothly along their splines, with no excessive looseness.

4. Check dog clutches for tooth wear. Worn clutch teeth may result in noise or jumping out of gear.

5. Place gears in neutral. Check that there is no interference between dog clutches and adjacent gears.

Installation

1. Install the output shaft, then the input shaft (refer to **Figure 127**).

> **CAUTION**
> *Be sure the input and output shafts are situated over their respective locating pins (**Figure 128**).*

2. Install the kickstarter spindle (**Figure 129**).

> **CAUTION**
> *Be sure the kickstarter spindle is situated over its locating pin (refer to **Figure 128**).*

3. Install the crankshaft and reassemble the crankcase halves, as outlined previously in this chapter.

SHIFT CAM AND SHIFT FORKS

The shift cam and shift forks (refer to **Figure 128**), together with the shifter mechanism, select various gear ratios within the transmission. Service is similar on all models.

Removal

1. Split the crankcase, and remove the crankshaft and transmission shafts as outlined previously in this chapter.

2. On the right side of the engine, remove screw holding shift drum and remove the C plate (**Figure 130**).

3. Remove guide pin clips and fish the shift fork guide pins out of their recesses with a piece of wire (refer to **Figure 128**).

4. Slide shift drum out (hold forks in one hand) as shown in **Figure 131**.

Inspection

1. Measure clearance between each shift fork and the shift drum. Replace shift forks and/or shift drum if clearance exceeds 0.006 in. (0.15mm).

2. Examine each shift fork for bending or evidence of rubbing on one side. Measure clearance between each shift fork and the groove on its associated gear. Any clearance greater than 0.025 in. (0.6mm) should be considered excessive. Replace the shift fork and/or gear if this situation exists.

Installation

1. Install the shift drum and shift forks in the crankcase. Use Loctite on all threads.

> NOTE: *Shift forks are marked R, C, and L, as you look at them as shown in* **Figure 128**. *(The right side of the engine is at the left of the photo, as the engine is upside down.)*

2. Install the shift fork guide pins in their recesses (refer to **Figure 128**).

> NOTE: *The shift fork guide pins are hollow. Be sure to install them with their solid end first.*

3. Install guide pin clips (refer to **Figure 128**).

4. Check to be sure that each shift fork is correctly installed, and that the clips do not interfere with the gears.

5. Install the transmission shafts and crankshaft, and reassemble the crankcase (refer to preceding sections for procedures).

FINAL ENGINE REASSEMBLY

Right Side of Engine

1. Install shifter mechanism (if removed). Refer to *Shifter Mechanism, Installation* section, this chapter.

2. Install clutch and oil pump (if removed). Refer to *Clutch and Oil Pump, Installation* section, this chapter.

3. Install the slotted nut that holds on the oil filter with a special tool available at your dealer (**Figure 132**).

4. Install the 6mm center screw for the oil filter (**Figure 133**).

5. Install the oil filter cap retaining screw (**Figure 134**).

6. Install the kickstarter spring (**Figure 135**).

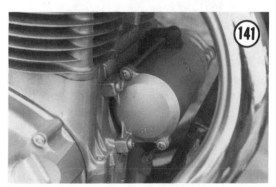

7. Install the crankcase cover (**Figure 136**).

8. Install the kickstarter lever (**Figure 137**).

Left Side of Engine

1. Install the starter sprocket and starter sprocket setting plate (**Figure 138**).

2. Install the alternator and alternator retaining nut (**Figure 139**).

3. Install sprocket and chain (**Figure 140**).

4. Push starter motor into case and install starter motor retaining screws (**Figure 141**).

5. Install neutral indicator switch (**Figure 142**).

6. Install clip holding alternator main wiring harness (**Figure 143**).

7. Install alternator cover (**Figure 144**).

8. Install shift lever (**Figure 145**).

ENGINE INSTALLATION

1. Set engine into frame.

2. Lift engine slightly, and install rear engine mounting bolts (**Figure 146**).

3. Install the front engine mounting bolts (**Figure 147**).

4. Install the cylinder head bracket and tighten bolts securely (**Figure 148**).

5. Connect condenser-to-coil wire (**Figure 149**).

6. Install starter cable in the clip that holds the cable under the starter (**Figure 150**), and in the clip behind the shift lever. Connect the starter cable to the starter cable connection (**Figure 151**) and push the boot firmly down over the connection.

7. Install the breather tube on the cylinder head (**Figure 152**).

8. Connect the alternator plug (**Figure 153**) and install a new tie-wrap.

9. Install the tachometer drive cable and secure with screw (**Figure 154**). Install the tachometer drive cover (**Figure 155**).

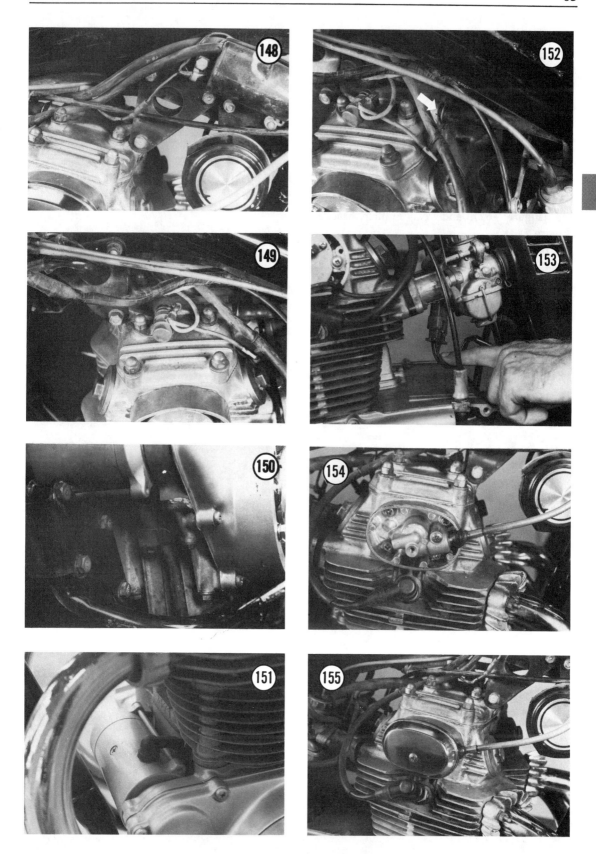

10. Install the alternator wiring (**Figure 156**).

11. Install countershaft sprocket (**Figure 157**).

12. Connect the clutch cable (**Figure 158**).

13. Install the countershaft sprocket cover (**Figure 159**).

14. Connect breaker point wire (**Figure 160**).

15. Install footpegs (**Figure 161**).

16. Install exhaust system (push collars into cylinder head and assemble all brackets).

17. Install exhaust pipe bracket above left footpeg (**Figure 162**), and rear muffler bracket (**Figure 153**).

18. Install spark plug leads in their clips (**Figure 164**).

19. Install exhaust pipe-to-cylinder head nuts (**Figure 165**).

20. Connect the carburetors to cylinder head (**Figure 166**).

21. Install gas tank.

22. Connect battery cable.

23. Connect fuel lines to fuel petcock (**Figure 167**).

4

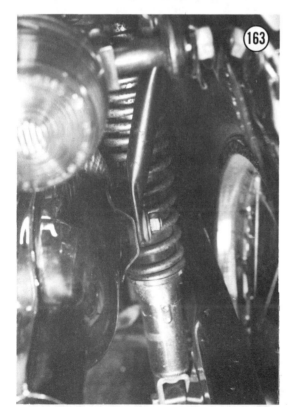

Final Checks

1. Install engine drain plug and fill with fresh engine oil.

2. Check engine mounting bolts for tightness as a final precaution.

3. Adjust the clutch, throttle cable, drive chain, ignition timing, and valves (refer to Chapter Two for procedures).

4. Inspect all nuts and bolts for tightness.

5. Check wiring for chafing or binding after engine installation.

CHAPTER FIVE

FUEL AND EXHAUST SYSTEMS

For proper operation, a gasoline engine must be supplied with fuel and air, mixed in proper proportions by weight. A mixture in which there is excess fuel is said to be rich. A lean mixture is one which contains insufficient fuel. It is the function of the carburetor to supply proper mixture to the engine under all operating conditions.

The Honda twins covered in this manual use a slide valve.

CARBURETOR OVERHAUL

There is no set rule regarding frequency of carburetor overhaul. A carburetor used on a machine used primarily for street riding may go 5,000 miles without attention. If the machine is used in dirt, the carburetor might need an overhaul in less than 1,000 miles. Poor engine performance, hesitation, and little or no response to idle mixture adjustment are all symptoms of possible carburetor malfunctions.

Removal/Installation

1. Remove the clamps and retaining nuts and lift the air cleaner (one on each side) off **(Figures 1 and 2)**.

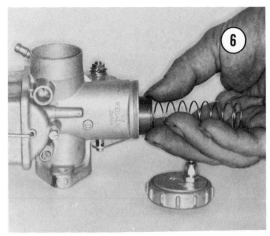

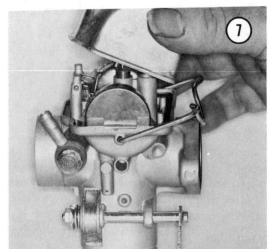

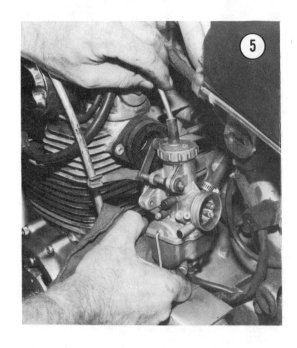

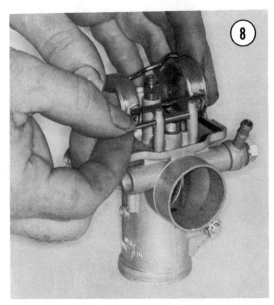

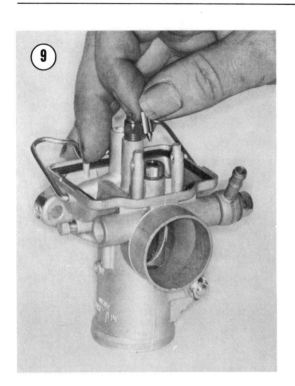

2. Remove carburetor clamps and intake hoses (**Figure 3**).

3. Disconnect throttle cables from throttle twist grip and loosen all routing clamps (**Figure 4**).

4. Remove carburetor assembly (with cables attached). See **Figure 5**.

5. Installation is the reverse of the preceding steps.

Disassembly/Assembly

1. Remove the cap, then pull out the throttle valve and spring (**Figure 6**).

2. Pull off the float bowl (**Figure 7**) after pushing its retaining bail out of the way.

3. Pull out the float pivot shaft, then gently remove the float (**Figure 8**). Take care not to bend the float arm during this operation.

4. Remove the float needle (**Figure 9**).

5. Remove the float valve seat (**Figure 10**). A

5

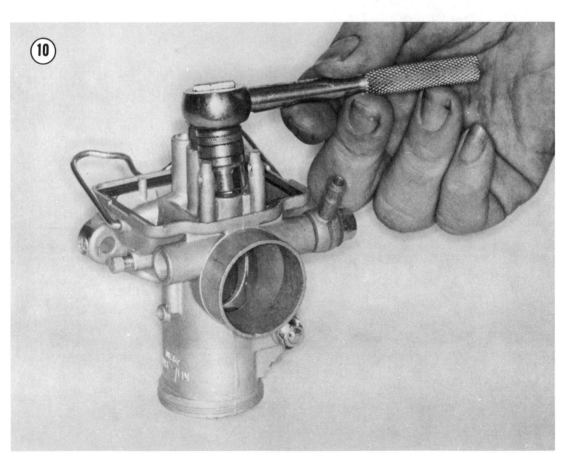

hooked wire may be used to remove its sealing washer.

6. Remove the needle jet holder and main jet together (**Figure 11**).

7. Push out the needle jet, using a plastic or fiber tool (**Figure 12**). Do not use any metal tool for this purpose.

8. Remove the pilot jet (**Figure 13**).

9. Remove the idle speed and idle mixture screws (**Figure 14**). Take care not to lose either spring.

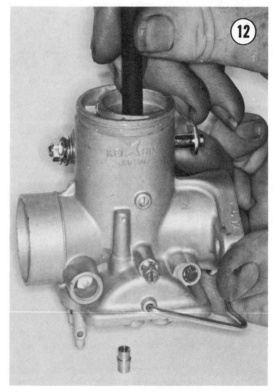

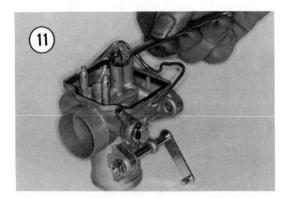

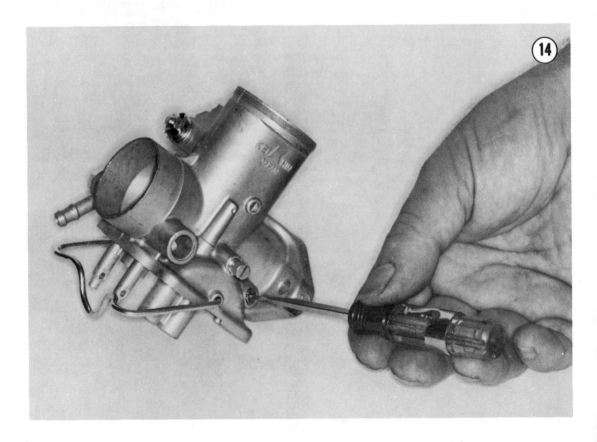

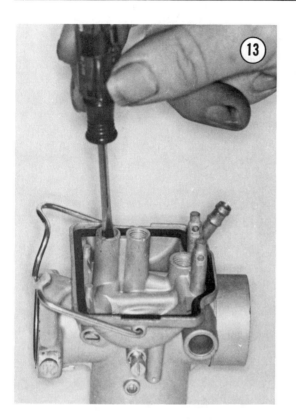

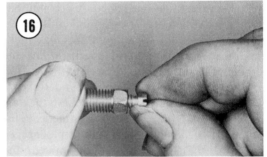

10. Disassemble the choke mechanism, if necessary, by removing the nut from the end of the choke lever shaft.

11. Remove O-ring from mounting flange.

12. Push the jet needle from the throttle slide (**Figure 15**). Do not lose the jet needle retaining clip. Upon reassembly, be sure that the retaining clip does not interfere with the slot in the throttle slide.

13. Separate the main jet from the needle jet holder (**Figure 16**).

14. Remove the drain screw from the float bowl.

5

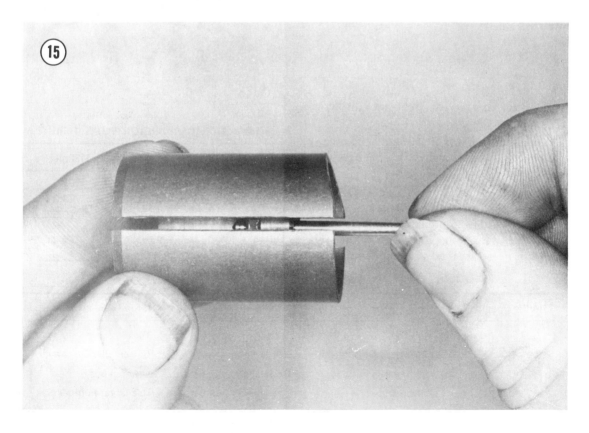

15. Remove fuel inlet banjo fitting **(Figure 17)**.

16. Reverse the preceding steps to assemble the carburetor. Always use new gasket and O-rings. Be sure to check float level before returning carburetor to service (refer to *Carburetor Adjustment,* following section).

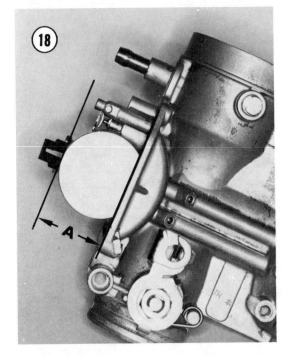

CARBURETOR ADJUSTMENT

The carburetor was designed to provide the proper mixture under all operating conditions. Little or no benefit will result from experimenting. However, unusual operating conditions such as sustained operation at high altitudes or unusually high or low temperatures may make modifications to standard specifications desirable. The adjustments described in the following paragraphs should only be undertaken if the rider has definite reason to believe they are required. Make the tests and adjustments in the order specified. Float level should be checked each time the carburetor is disassembled, and adjusted if necessary.

A summary of carburetor adjustments is given in **Table 1**.

Float Level

To check carburetor float level, refer to **Figure 18**.

1. Tilt the carburetor slowly until the tang on the float just barely touches the float needle.

2. Measure the distance between the bottom of the float and the bottom surface of the carburetor body **(Figure 18)**. This distance must be as specified in **Table 2**, and equal for both floats. Bend the tang on the float arm **(Figure 19)** as necessary if adjustment is required.

Table 2   CARBURETOR FLOAT HEIGHT

Model	Inches	Millimeters
125	0.93	21.0
CD175	1.09	28.0
160	0.77	19.5
All other 175 and 200	0.83	21.0

Table 1   CARBURETOR ADJUSTMENT SUMMARY

Throttle Opening	Adjustment	If too Rich	If too Lean
0 - 1/8	Air screw	Turn out	Turn in
1/8 - 1/4	Throttle valve cutaway	Use larger cutaway	Use smaller cutaway
1/4 - 3/4	Jet needle	Raise clip	Lower clip
3/4 - full	Main jet	Use smaller number	Use larger number

Table 3   POOR MIXTURE SYMPTOMS

Condition	Symptom
Rich mixture	Rough idle
	Black exhaust smoke
	Hard starting, especially when hot
	Black deposits in exhaust pipes
	Gas-fouled spark plugs
	Poor gas mileage
	Engine performs worse as it warms up
Lean mixture	Backfiring
	Rough idle
	Overheating
	Hesitation upon acceleration
	Engine speed varies at fixed throttle
	Loss of power
	White color on spark plug insulators
	Poor acceleration

BEND TANG TO ADJUST FLOAT LEVEL

Jet Size

Make a road test at full throttle for final determination of main jet size. To make such a test, operate the motorcycle at full throttle for at least 2 minutes, then shut the engine off, release the clutch, and bring the machine to a stop.

If at full throttle, the engine runs "heavily," the main jet is too large. If the engine runs better by closing the throttle slightly, the main jet is too small. The engine will run at full throttle evenly and regularly if the main jet is of the correct size.

After each such test, remove and examine the spark plugs. The insulators should have a light tan color. If the insulators have black sooty deposits, the mixture is too rich. If there are signs of intense heat, such as a blistered white appearance, the mixture is too lean.

As a general rule, main jet size should be reduced approximately 5% for each 3,000 feet (1,000 meters) above sea level.

Table 3 lists symptoms caused by rich and lean mixtures.

Idle Speed and Mixture Adjustment

1. Start engine and allow it to warm to operating temperature, then shut it off.

2. Turn each idle mixture screw in until it seats

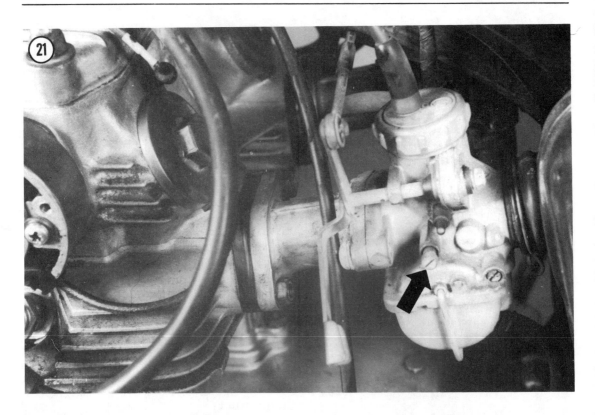

lightly, then back out each one 1¼ turns (**Figure 20**).

3. Start the engine. Adjust each idle speed screw so that the engine idles at 1,000-2,000 rpm (**Figure 21**).

4. Place one hand behind each muffler and adjust idle speed screw (refer to **Figure 21**) until exhaust pressure from each muffler is equal.

5. Turn left cylinder idle mixture screw in either direction, slowly, until engine idle speed is at its maximum.

6. Repeat Step 5 for the right cylinder.

7. Check exhaust pressure from each cylinder (as in Step 4) and adjust either idle speed screw necessary to equalize pressure.

8. Turn each idle speed screw an equal amount to obtain 1,000-1,200 rpm idle speed.

9. Synchronize both carburetors. See *Synchronizing the Carburetors*.

If the preceding procedure does not work well, due to both carburetors being too far out of adjustment, use the following procedure:

1. Turn the idle mixture screw on each carburetor in until it seats lightly, then back it out 1¼ turns (refer to **Figure 20**).

2. Start the engine, then ride the bike long enough to warm it thoroughly.

3. Stop the engine and disconnect either spark plug lead.

4. Restart the engine on one cylinder. Turn the idle speed screw on the "working" carburetor in enough to keep the engine running (refer to **Figure 21**).

5. Turn the idle speed screw out until the engine runs slower and begins to falter.

6. Turn the idle mixture screw in or out to make the engine run smoothly. Note the speed indicated by the tachometer.

7. Repeat Steps 5 and 6 to achieve the lowest possible stable idle speed.

8. Stop the engine, then reconnect the spark plug lead that was disconnected.

9. Repeat Steps 3 through 8 for the other cylinder, matching the engine speed with that observed in Step 6.

10. Start the engine, then turn each idle speed screw an equal amount until the engine idles at 1,000-1,200 rpm.

11. Place one hand behind each muffler and check that the exhaust pressures are equal. If

not, turn either idle speed screw in or out until they are.

12. Adjust carburetor synchronization (see following procedure).

Synchronizing the Carburetors

1. Twist the throttle grip and see if both throttle slides begin to move upward at the same time (**Figure 22**).

2. If throttle slides need adjusting, turn the cable adjuster at the top of either carburetor until the slides move together perfectly (**Figure 23**).

> NOTE: *A small mirror may be helpful during this check.*

MISCELLANEOUS CARBURETOR PROBLEMS

Water in carburetor float bowls and sticking carburetor slide valves can result from careless washing of the motorcycle. To remedy this problem, remove and clean the carburetor bowl, main jet, and any other affected parts. Be sure to cover the air intake when washing the machine.

If gasoline leaks past the float bowl gasket, high speed fuel starvation may occur. Varnish deposits on the outside of the float bowl are evidence of this condition.

Dirt in the fuel may be lodged in the float valve and cause an overrich mixture. As a temporary measure, tap the carburetor lightly with any convenient tool to dislodge the dirt. Clean the fuel tank, petcock, fuel line, and carburetor at the first opportunity, should this situation occur.

CARBURETOR SPECIFICATIONS

Table 4 lists major specifications of carburetors of the more popular bikes covered by this manual. These specifications have been determined by exhaustive factory tests, and should not be changed unless there is good reason for doing so.

Table 4   CARBURETOR JETS

Model	Pilot Jet	Main Jet
CB125	35	62
CA160	42	98
CB160	38	90
CL160	38	95 or 98
CD175	40	98
CB175 (inclined cylinder)	35	95
CB175 (vertical cylinders)	38	98
CL175 (inclined cylinders)	38	98
CL175 (vertical cylinders)	38	90
SL175	38	92
CB200	38	88
CL200	35	95

FUEL TANK

Removal/Installation

1. Loosen seat mounting bolts, then remove the seat (**Figure 24**).

2. Be sure that the fuel flow is shut off at the petcock, then remove fuel lines at petcock (**Figure 25**).

3. Detach fuel tank from its rear rubber mount; lift it upward and to the rear. Be sure that no wires catch on the tank as it is removed (**Figure 26**).

4. Reverse preceding steps to install the fuel tank.

Inspection

1. Be sure that the filler cap vent is not clogged.

2. Check all rubber mounts, and replace them if they are damaged.

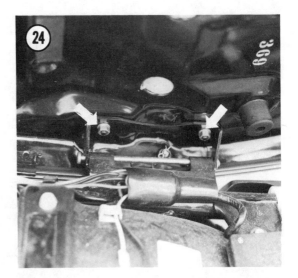

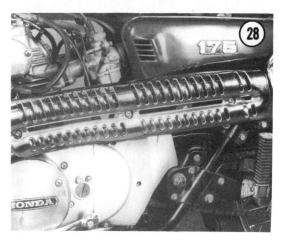

3. Check fuel lines for leaks, hardening, or cracks.

4. Check for sediment in the tank, and flush out if necessary.

> WARNING
> *Open flames, cigarettes, water heater or clothes dryer pilot lights, or electrical sparks may trigger a fatal explosion. Do not work on any fuel system component within 50 feet of any possible source of ignition.*

Fuel Strainer Service

The fuel strainer filters out particles which might otherwise get into a carburetor and cause the float needle valve to remain open, resulting in flooding. Such particles might also get into the engine and cause damage.

Remove the fuel strainer, located at the fuel petcock (refer to **Figure 25**), and clean it in solvent, then blow dry with compressed air. Be sure that all gaskets are in good condition upon reassembly.

EXHAUST SYSTEM

Removal/Installation

1. Remove nuts at each cylinder head (**Figure 27**).

2. Remove footpegs and footrest bar if necessary (**Figure 28**).

3. Remove rear attachment bolts (**Figure 29**).

4. Reverse preceding steps to install the exhaust system.

Inspection

1. Check gaskets and rubber cushions for cracks or damage.

2. Pull out baffle tubes (if so equipped) and remove carbon deposits.

CHAPTER SIX

ELECTRICAL SYSTEM

This chapter covers operating principles and removal and installation procedures for Honda ignition and electrical systems. Refer to Chapter Two for tune-up procedures; refer to Chapter Three for troubleshooting procedures.

IGNITION SYSTEM

Honda twin-cylinder models are equipped with a battery and coil ignition system, similar in many ways to a conventional automobile.

Circuit Operation

Figure 1 illustrates a typical battery ignition system for a single cylinder. When the breaker points are closed, current flows from the battery through the primary windings of the ignition coil, thereby building a magnetic field around the coil. The breaker cam rotates at one-half crankshaft speed and is so adjusted that the breaker points open as the piston reaches firing position.

As the points open, the magnetic field collapses. When this happens, a very high voltage is induced (up to approximately 15,000 volts) in the secondary winding of the ignition coil. This high voltage is sufficient to jump the gap at the spark plug.

The condenser assists the coil in developing high voltage, and also protects the points. In-

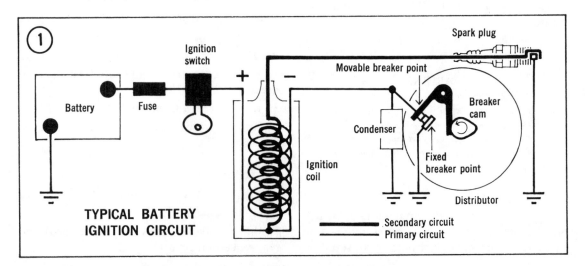

TYPICAL BATTERY IGNITION CIRCUIT

ductance of the ignition coil primary winding tends to keep a surge of current flowing through the circuit even after the points have started to open. The condenser stores this surge and thus prevents arcing at the points. Each end of the coil secondary winding connects to a spark plug, and so both spark plugs fire simultaneously. This is possible because as one plug fires at the end of a compression stroke, the other plug fires at the end of an exhaust stroke.

Troubleshooting

Refer to Chapter Three, for any problems related to the electrical system.

Ignition Coil

The ignition coil is a transformer which develops the high voltage required to jump the spark plug gap. The only maintenance required is that of keeping the electrical connections clean and tight, and occasionally checking to see that the coil is mounted securely (**Figure 2**).

Service

There are two major items requiring service on battery ignition models: breaker point service and ignition timing. Both are vitally important to proper engine operation and reliability. Refer to Chapter Two, *Breaker Points* and *Ignition Timing* sections.

CHARGING SYSTEM

The charging system on all Honda twins covered by this manual consists of an alternator, battery, and interconnecting wiring. Some models are also equipped with a solid state voltage regulator.

Alternator

An alternator is an alternating current electrical generator in which a magnetized field rotor revolves within a set of stationary coils called a stator. As the rotor revolves, alternating current is induced in the stator. Stator current is then rectified and used to operate electrical accessories on the motorcycle and for battery charging. Refer to **Figure 3**.

Removal/Installation

1. Remove shift lever **(Figure 4)**.

2. Remove alternator cover screws **(Figure 5)** and tap cover off with a rubber mallet **(Figure 6)**.

3. Remove clip holding alternator main wiring harness **(Figure 7)**.

4. Remove neutral indicator switch **(Figure 8)**.

5. Remove alternator retaining nut and pull alternator with a suitable puller **(Figure 9)**.

6. Install by reversing the preceding steps.

Rectifier

All models are equipped with a full-wave bridge rectifier **(Figure 10)**.

> *CAUTION*
> *Always handle the rectifier assembly carefully. Do not bend or try to rotate the wafers. Do not loosen the screws which hold the assembly together. Moisture can damage the assembly, so keep it dry. Never run the engine with the battery disconnected or without a fuse; doing so can cause immediate rectifier destruction.*

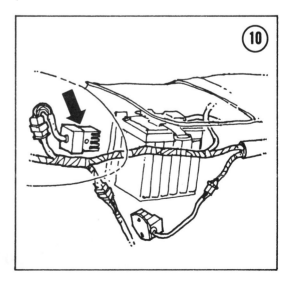

Voltage Regulator

Problems with this unit rarely occur. Refer to Chapter Three for test procedures for the voltage regulator should this unit be suspected of causing trouble **(Figure 11)**.

> CAUTION
> *Do not connect or disconnect the regulator with the engine running.*

ELECTRIC STARTER

Refer to **Figure 12** for a diagram of a typical starting system.

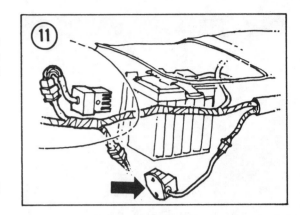

Starter Motor

The starter motor **(Figure 13)** is wound in series for high torque, and draws approximately 120 amperes under normal starting conditions. This figure can vary considerably, depending on engine temperature, starter condition, and other factors.

Removal/Installation

1. Remove shift lever **(Figure 14)**.
2. Remove alternator cover screws **(Figure 15)** and tap cover off with a rubber mallet **(Figure 16)**.

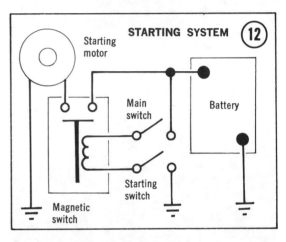

STARTING SYSTEM

Starting motor

Main switch

Battery

Starting switch

Magnetic switch

3. Remove starter motor retaining screws (**Figure 17**) and tap starter motor out of case (rearward) with a rubber mallet (**Figure 18**).

4. Remove chain and sprocket (**Figure 19**).

5. Remove starter sprocket setting plate (**Figure 20**), then remove starter sprocket (if necessary).

6. Install by reversing the preceding steps.

LIGHTS

The headlight assembly consists primarily of a headlight lens and reflector unit, rim, and related hardware.

In the event of lighting problems, first check the affected bulb. Poor ground connections are another cause of lamp malfunctions.

Turn signals usually operate from direct current supplied by the battery. When replacing the signal bulbs, always be sure to use the proper type. Erratic operation or even failure to flash may result from use of wrong bulbs.

Stoplights usually operate from direct current also. Stoplight switches should be adjusted so that the lamp comes on just before braking action begins. Front brake stoplight switches are frequently built into the front brake cable, and are not adjustable.

HEADLIGHT

Replacement

Refer to **Figure 21**.

1. Remove 3 screws and remove headlight from case.

2. Disconnect socket from sealed beam.

3. Remove 2 retaining lock pins and screws from rim.

4. Remove sealed beam.

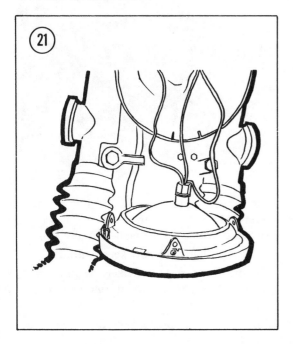

5. Installation is the reverse of these steps. Adjust headlight as described below.

Adjustment

Adjust headlight horizontally and vertically, according to Department of Motor Vehicle regulations in your state.

To adjust headlight horizontally, turn the screw illustrated in **Figure 22**. To adjust vertically, loosen the bolts on either side of the case. Move the headlight to the desired position, then tighten bolts.

TAIL/STOPLIGHTS

Taillight Replacement

A single bulb performs as a taillight, license plate light, and stoplight. To replace the bulb, remove the lens and turn bulb counterclockwise.

HORN

Figure 23 is a typical horn circuit. Current for the horn is supplied by the battery. One terminal is connected to the battery through the main switch. The other terminal is grounded when the horn button is pressed.

BATTERY SERVICE

Honda motorcycles are equipped with lead-

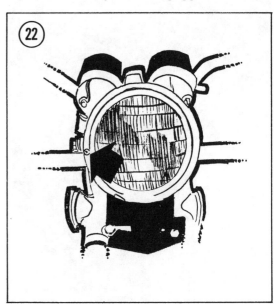

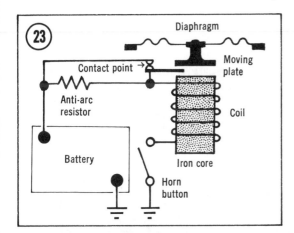

acid storage batteries, smaller in size but similar in construction, to batteries used in automobiles (**Figure 24**).

Refer to Chapter Two, *Battery* section, for maintenance procedures.

WIRING DIAGRAMS

Reference to the following wiring diagrams will make electrical system troubleshooting easier.

Refer to Chapter Three for troubleshooting procedures.

6

Wiring diagrams follow on pages 88-94.

WIRING DIAGRAM — CB125 (U.K.)

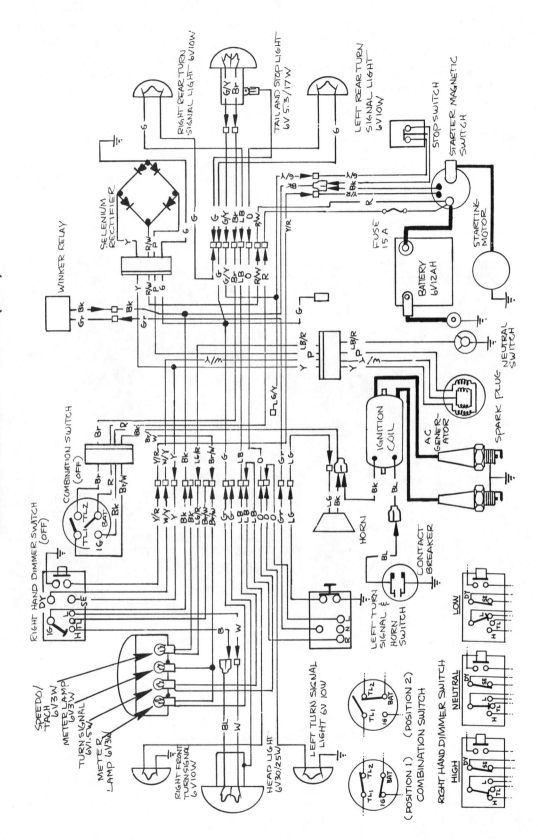

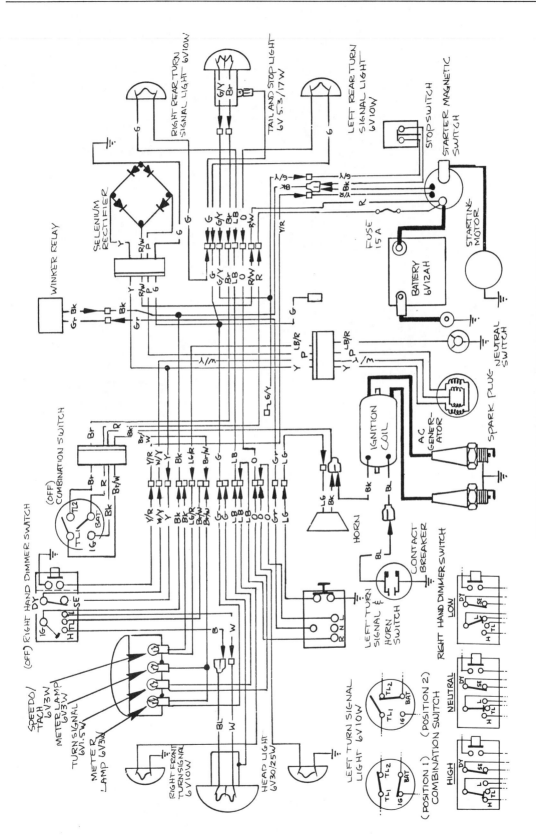

WIRING DIAGRAM — CD125 AND SS125A

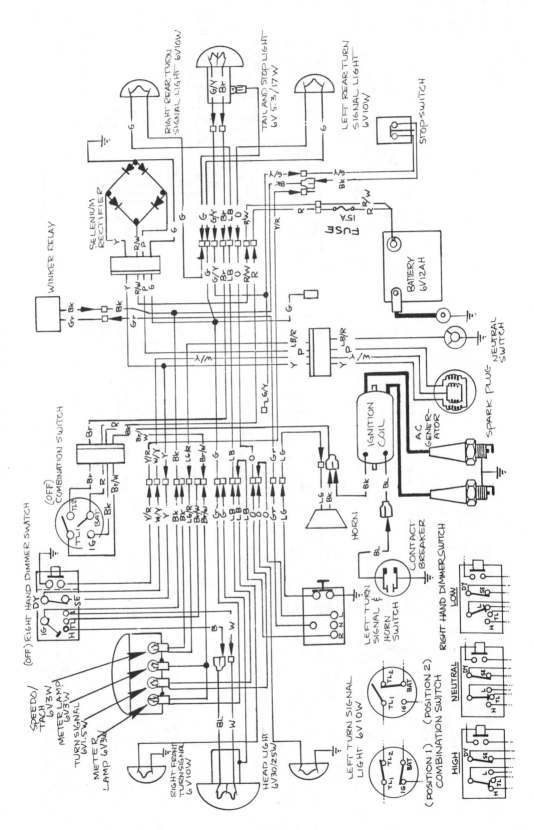

WIRING DIAGRAM – CL125

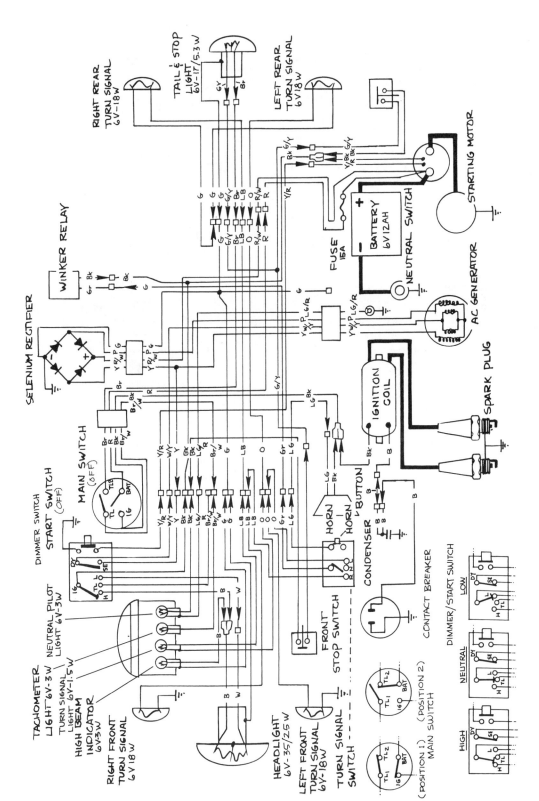

WIRING DIAGRAM — CA/CD175

6

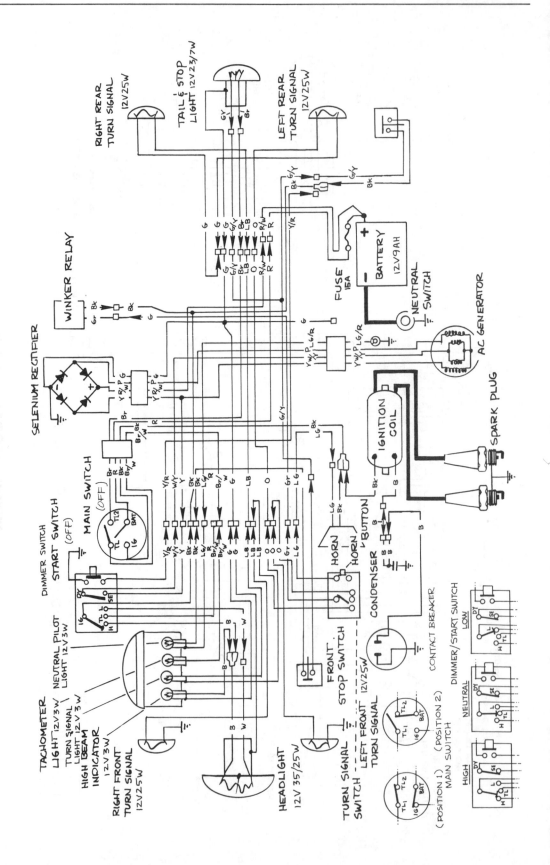

WIRING DIAGRAM — CL175

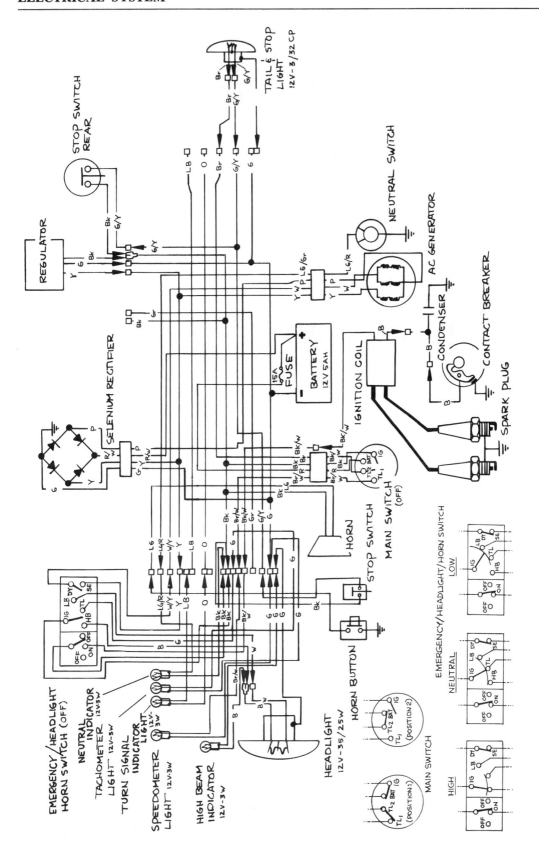

WIRING DIAGRAM — SL175 (U.K.)

6

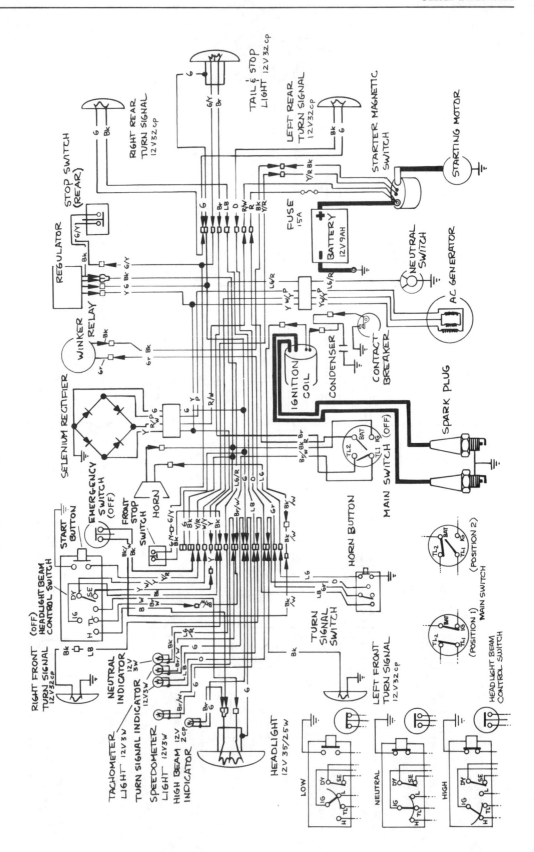

WIRING DIAGRAM — CB200 AND CL200

CHAPTER SEVEN

FRAME, SUSPENSION, AND STEERING

This chapter provides all service procedures for the wheels, brakes, chassis, and related components.

HANDLEBAR

Most manual controls are mounted on the handlebar assembly. Wiring from switches is routed to the headlight, where it is connected to the main wiring harness.

Removal

1. Disconnect front brake cable (**Figure 1**) and clutch cables (**Figure 2**) at their respective levers.

2. Disconnect the throttle cable at the throttle grip (**Figure 3**).

3. Remove the headlight assembly (**Figure 4**), then disconnect all wiring from the handlebar.

4. Remove bolts and handlebar clamps. See **Figure 5**.

5. Lift handlebar from fork top bridge.

Inspection

1. Check cables for chafed or kinked housings. Grease inner cables and be sure that cables operate smoothly.

2. Twist throttle grip. Operation should be smooth throughout its entire travel.

3. Check both hand levers for smooth operation.

4. Check handlebar tubing for cracks or bends.

5. Check switches for proper operation.

6. Inspect wiring for chafed or frayed insulation. Be sure wire terminals are clean and free from corrosion.

Installation

Reverse the *Removal* procedures to install the handlebar. Observe the following notes.

1. Be sure control cables are routed so that they will not be pinched at any position of the front end assembly.

2. Check cables for free movement.

3. Be sure wiring is connected properly.

4. Adjust clutch, front brake, and throttle cables after handlebar service. Refer to Chapter Two for procedures.

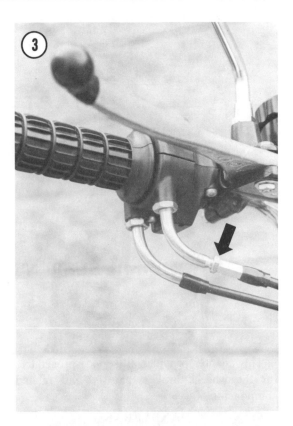

FORK TOP BRIDGE

The fork top bridge is mounted on top of the front fork assembly and is retained by the steering stem nut (**Figure 6**).

Removal

1. Remove the handlebar assembly (refer to *Handlebar, Removal*, preceding section).

2. Remove steering damper (if so equipped). See **Figure 7**.

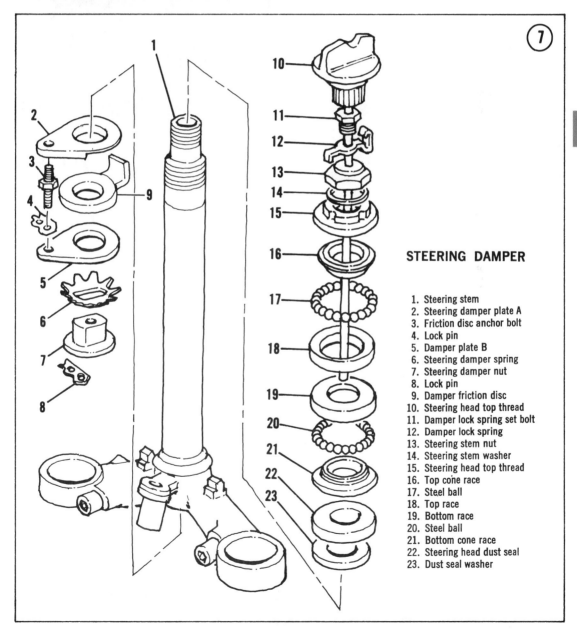

STEERING DAMPER

1. Steering stem
2. Steering damper plate A
3. Friction disc anchor bolt
4. Lock pin
5. Damper plate B
6. Steering damper spring
7. Steering damper nut
8. Lock pin
9. Damper friction disc
10. Steering head top thread
11. Damper lock spring set bolt
12. Damper lock spring
13. Steering stem nut
14. Steering stem washer
15. Steering head top thread
16. Top cone race
17. Steel ball
18. Top race
19. Bottom race
20. Steel ball
21. Bottom cone race
22. Steering head dust seal
23. Dust seal washer

3. Disconnect speedometer and tachometer cables (**Figure 8**).

4. Remove front fork top bolts and steering stem nut (**Figure 9**).

5. If so equipped, remove nuts, washers, cushions, and handlebar holders (**Figure 10**).

Inspection

Check for cracks or other damage, and replace worn cushions.

Installation

Reverse the *Removal* procedure, this section, to install the fork top bridge. Observe all notes under *Handlebar, Installation*, Steps 1-4.

STEERING STEM

The steering stem is supported by ball bearings at both ends which enable it to pivot in the frame headpipe (**Figure 11**). Most machines incorporate a steering damper (refer to **Figure 7**).

Removal

1. Remove handlebar (refer to *Handlebar* section, this chapter).

2. Remove front wheel (refer to *Wheels* section, this chapter).

3. Remove both front fork legs (refer to *Front Fork* section, this chapter).

4. Remove front fork top bridge (refer to *Fork Top Bridge*, preceding section).

5. Remove steering stem nut (**Figure 12**), then carefully withdraw steering stem downward from frame headpipe (**Figure 13**).

> NOTE: *Be careful not to drop any steel balls.*

Inspection

Examine balls and races for cracks, chips, wear, or other damage. Be sure that dust seals are in good condition. Check for damaged threads. Refer to **Figure 14**.

> NOTE: *Never use any combination of new and used bearings. Replace bear-*

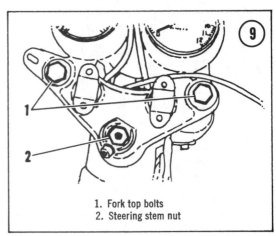

1. Fork top bolts
2. Steering stem nut

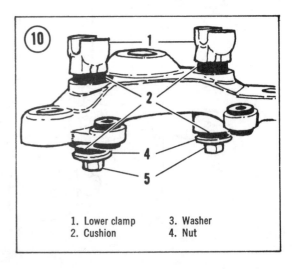

1. Lower clamp   3. Washer
2. Cushion   4. Nut

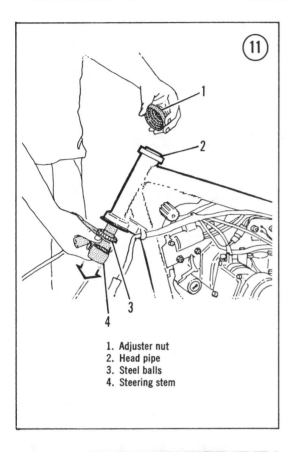

1. Adjuster nut
2. Head pipe
3. Steel balls
4. Steering stem

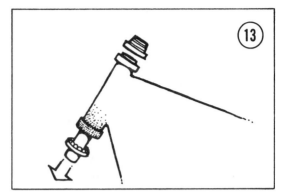

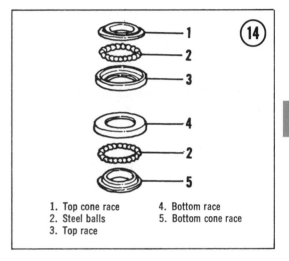

1. Top cone race   4. Bottom race
2. Steel balls   5. Bottom cone race
3. Top race

ings as complete sets if any defects are found.

Installation

1. Clean bearings in solvent, then dry and lubricate.

> NOTE: *Be careful not to drop any steel balls. Heavy grease will hold them during assembly.*

2. Insert the steering stem upward into the frame headpipe and thread the steering stem nut on. Tighten the nut enough so that the steering stem turns freely without looseness or binding. Refer to **Figure 12**.

WHEELS

Front Wheel Removal/Installation

1. Place a suitable stand under the frame so that the front wheel is off the ground.

7

2. Unfasten lockwasher and remove hex nut holding the brake stopper arm (**Figure 15**).

3. Remove fork end cap nuts (**Figure 16**).

4. Remove speedometer drive screw (**Figure 17**) and pull out speedometer cable (**Figure 18**).

5. Remove cotter pin and disconnect front cable (**Figures 19 and 20**).

6. Remove fork end cap nuts and fork end cap on other side (**Figure 21**) and remove wheel.

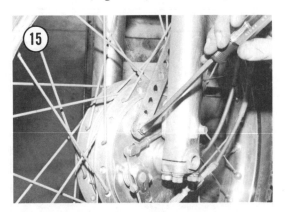

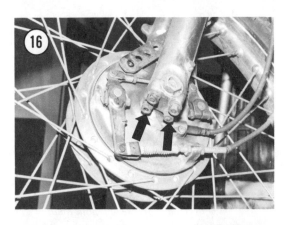

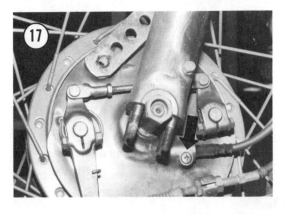

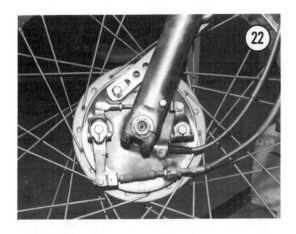

7. Install the wheel by reversing the preceding steps.

8. With the front wheel still supported off the ground, adjust the front brake (refer to **Figure 22** for the following sequence):

    a. Loosen locknut.

    b. Turn adjuster nut to obtain desired braking action.

    c. Tighten locknut.

Rear Wheel Removal/Installation

1. Remove master link and chain (**Figure 23**).

2. Remove wire safety clip on rear brake torque link (**Figure 24**).

3. Remove nut and washer and remove rear brake torque link (**Figure 25**).

4. On other side, remove cotter pin, axle nut, and washer (**Figure 26**).

5. Remove brake adjusting nut and disconnect brake cable (**Figure 27**).

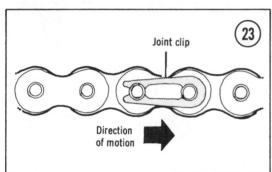

Joint clip

Direction of motion

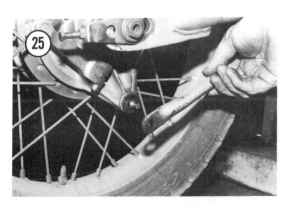

6. Drive axle shaft out (**Figure 28**).

7. Pull wheel out to the rear (**Figure 29**).

8. To install rear wheel, perform the following steps:

   a. Insert wheel spacer (**Figure 30**).

   b. On other side, align axle and axle hole. Insert spacer and slide axle shaft in (grease it first). See **Figure 31**.

   c. Lightly tighten the axle nuts (**Figure 32**).

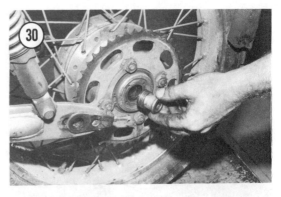

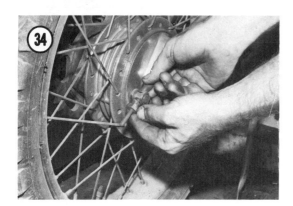

d. Connect rear brake torque link with a washer and nut and install cotter pin (**Figure 33**).

e. Install chain. Be sure master link is installed exactly as shown in **Figure 23**.

f. Refer to **Figure 34**. Connect brake cable and thread brake adjusting nut on to rod. Turn each adjustment bolt (one on each side of wheel) until there is ¾-1 in. (20-25mm) of up and down movement in the center of the lower chain run (**Figure 35**). Tighten the locknut (one on each side of wheel).

NOTE: *Be sure that the reference marks on the swinging arm and the index marks on the chain adjuster are in the same relative position on each side (refer to* **Figure 34**).

g. Tighten the rear axle nuts and install new cotter pins (refer to **Figure 36**).

9. To adjust the rear brake, turn the adjusting nut (**Figure 37**) until the rear brake pedal has

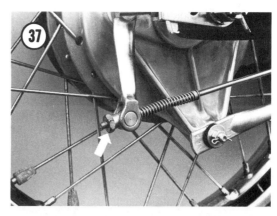

approximately ¾-1 in. (20-25mm) of free play (**Figure 38**).

Wheel Inspection

1. Refer to **Figure 39**. Mount the wheel so that a dial indicator can measure wheel rim runout. Observe the dial indicator while rotating the wheel. Runout limit for all models is 0.08 in. (2.0mm).

2. Check axles for bends by supporting each by its center in a V-block, then rotating the shaft. Measure runout at each end with dial indicators. Replace any axle which is bent more than 0.008 in. (0.2mm).

3. Check wheel bearings for cracks, galling, or pitting. Rotate them by hand to check for roughness. Replace bearings if they are worn or damaged. If bearings are satisfactory, clean them in solvent, dry thoroughly, and repack with fresh wheel bearing grease.

4. Check rear wheel shock absorbers for wear. Replace if worn or damaged.

5. Check spokes for looseness or bending. A bent or otherwise faulty spoke will affect neighboring ones, and should be replaced immediately. Refer to information under *Spokes*, later on in this section.

6. Inspect oil seals for wear or damage. Replace if there is any doubt about condition.

7. Check rims for bending or distortion.

Wheel Balance

An unbalanced wheel results in unsafe riding conditions. Depending on the degree of unbalance and speed of the motorcycle, the rider may experience anything from a mild vibration to a violent shimmy which may even result in loss of control. Balance weights may be installed to spokes on the light side of the wheel to correct this condition.

Before attempting to balance wheels, check to be sure that the wheel bearings are in good condition and properly lubricated. Also make sure that brakes do not drag, so that wheels rotate freely.

With the wheel free of the ground, spin it slowly and allow it to come to rest by itself.

Add balance weights to the spokes on the light side as required, so that the wheel comes to rest at a different position each time. Balance weights are available in weights of 10, 20, and 30 grams. Remove the drive chain before balancing rear wheel.

If more than one ounce is required to balance the wheel, add weight to adjacent spokes; never put two or more weights on the same spoke. When the wheel comes to rest at a different point each time the wheel is spun, consider it balanced and tightly crimp the weights so they will not be thrown off.

Spokes

Spokes should be checked for tightness. The "tuning fork" method of checking spoke tightness is simple and works well. Tap each spoke with a spoke wrench or shank of a screwdriver and listen to the tone. A tightened spoke will emit a clear, ringing tone, and a loose spoke will sound flat. All spokes in a correctly tightened wheel will emit tones of similar pitch but not necessarily the same precise tone.

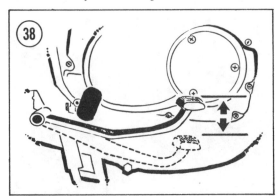

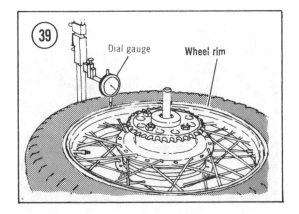

Dial gauge   Wheel rim

Bent or stripped spokes should be replaced as soon as they are detected. Unscrew the nipple from the spoke and depress the nipple into the rim far enough to free the end of the spoke, taking care not to push the spoke all the way in. Remove the damaged spoke from the hub and use it to match a new spoke of identical length.

If necessary, trim the new spoke to match the original and dress the end of the threads with a die. Install the new spoke in the hub and screw on the nipple, tightening it until the spoke's tone is similar to the tone of the other spokes on the wheel. Periodically check the new spoke; it will stretch and must be retightened several times before it takes its final set.

FRONT FORK

The front fork assembly serves as a shock absorber for the front wheel. Each leg consists of a spring and oil damper contained within telescoping tubes.

Removal

1. Place a pan under each fork leg, then remove drain plug at lower end of each fork leg and allow oil to drain out into pan (**Figure 40**).

> NOTE: *To aid in removing all of the oil, push down on the forks several times to force oil out.*

2. Remove front wheel (refer to *Wheels*, preceding section).

3. Loosen top fork crown pinch bolts (**Figure 41**).

4. Loosen lower fork crown pinch bolts (**Figure 42**).

7

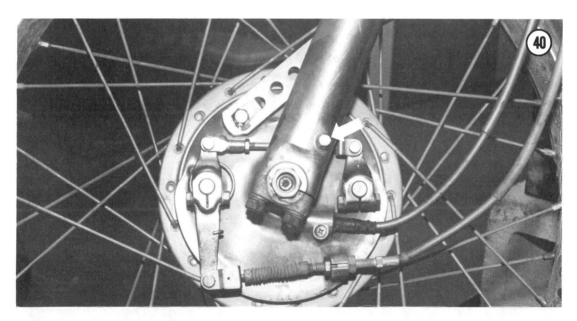

5. With a twisting motion, pull fork downward and out (**Figure 43**).

Disassembly/Assembly

1. Remove top fork bolt (**Figure 44**).

2. Remove rubber dust cover (**Figure 45**).

3. Remove circlip to release seal (**Figure 46**).

4. Loosen Allen screw in base of fork (**Figure 47**).

5. Gently pry seal out (**Figure 48**).

6. Drive in new seal with a suitable drift or a socket (**Figure 49**).

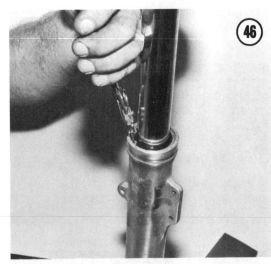

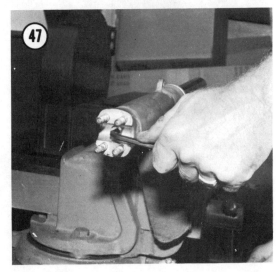

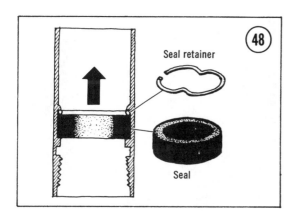

Seal retainer

Seal

NOTE: *Be sure that the oil seals are in good condition; replace if in doubt. Any roughness on the upper tube where it passes through the oil seal will cause rapid failure upon reassembly.*

7. To assemble, reverse the preceding steps.

Installation

1. Install the fork by reversing the steps listed under *Removal*, this section.

2. Fill the forks by pouring fresh fork oil through the top fork bolt hole (**Figure 50**). Refer to **Table 1**.

Table 1   FORK OIL QUANTITY

Model	Ounces	Cubic Centimeters
125 and 160	5.7	170
CB175, CL175	4.5-4.8	135-145
SL175	5.8-6.2	175-185
200	4.3-4.5	128-132

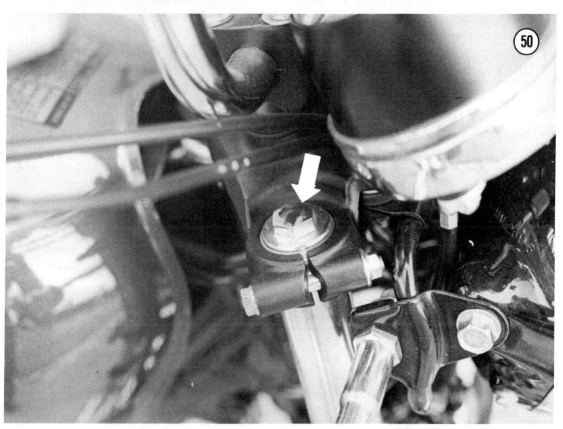

BRAKES

Drum brakes are standard on the rear of all Honda Twins covered in this manual. Most models have drum brakes as standard equipment on the front wheel; a few use a mechanically-actuated front disc brake. Service procedures for both are given.

Adjust brakes every 1,000 miles (1,500 kilometers), or whenever necessary.

Drum Brake (Front and Rear Wheel)

Brake service is similar for front and rear wheels.

1. Remove front or rear wheel (refer to *Wheels* section, this chapter).

2. On front wheel, remove axle nut (**Figure 51**) and slide brake assembly out (**Figure 52**). On rear wheel, pull brake assembly out as shown in **Figure 53**.

3. Measure the brake drum inner diameter with a vernier caliper (**Figure 54**). Replace if brake drum is worn beyond service limits recommended in **Table 2**. Also measure brake lining thickness and replace if worn to less than the wear limits specified in **Table 3**.

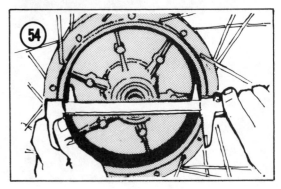

Table 2   BRAKE DRUM SERVICE LIMITS

Model	Service Limits	
	Inches	Millimeters
125 and 160	6.77	172
175		
Front	6.38	162
Rear	5.59	142
200		
Front	6.34	161
Rear	5.55	141

Table 3   BRAKE LINING WEAR LIMITS

Model	Wear Limit	
	Inches	Millimeters
125 and 160	0.08	2.0
175	0.16	4.0
200		
Front	0.08	2.0
Rear	0.06	1.5

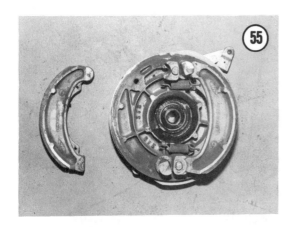

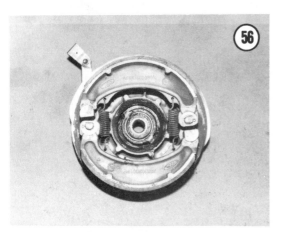

4. To replace brake shoes, refer to **Figure 55**. Remove the cotter pin, washer, springs, and brake shoes. Reverse disassembly procedure to reassemble the brake assembly.

> NOTE: *If brake arms have been removed, be sure that the punch marks on the brake arm align with corresponding mark on brake cam.*

5. **Figure 56** shows the brake completely assembled from the front; **Figure 57**, from the back.

6. Reverse Steps 1 and 2, preceding, to install the brake assemblies and wheels.

> NOTE: *When installing the front brake assembly in the hub, be sure that the slots match up. See **Figure 58**.*

7. Adjust the brakes (refer to *Brake Adjust-ment*, this chapter).

Front Disc Brake
(Mechanically-Actuated)

1. Wash all dirt from brake assembly with clean water.

2. Refer to **Figure 59**. Push cable boot up to expose the cable adjuster. Turn the adjuster all the way in.

3. Remove 3 bolts holding caliper cover in place (refer to **Figure 59**).

4. Remove brake cable from brake arm (**Figure 60**). No further disassembly is necessary to replace the brake pads. Wrap the brake arm with a clean rag to protect it from dirt.

5. Refer to **Figure 61**. Remove thrust plate guide and install a 6mm bolt into the threaded hole of outer brake pad. Pull the pad out.

6. Support the motorcycle so that the front wheel is clear. Remove the front wheel.

7. Refer to **Figure 62**. Remove the inner brake pad while you press on the lock pin with a screwdriver. This pad should be removed from the same side as the outer brake pad, but if it is worn to the red warning line, it can be removed from the disc side.

8. Replace brake pads if they are worn to their red warning lines.

9. Wipe all caliper sliding surfaces with solvent. Remove all dirt.

10. Apply a small quantity of silicone grease to the back side of inner brake pad, then install it (refer to **Figure 62**).

11. Install a new O-ring on the outer brake pad, then apply a very small quantity of silicone grease to its circumference and install it so that its mark aligns with matching mark on the caliper body (**Figure 63**).

12. Connect the brake cable end to the brake arm. Install the thrust plate guide (refer to **Figure 61**).

13. Disengage ratchet from brake arm and turn out adjusting bolt until it seats lightly. See **Figures 64 and 65**.

> NOTE: *Disregard this operation if only the brake cable is replaced.*

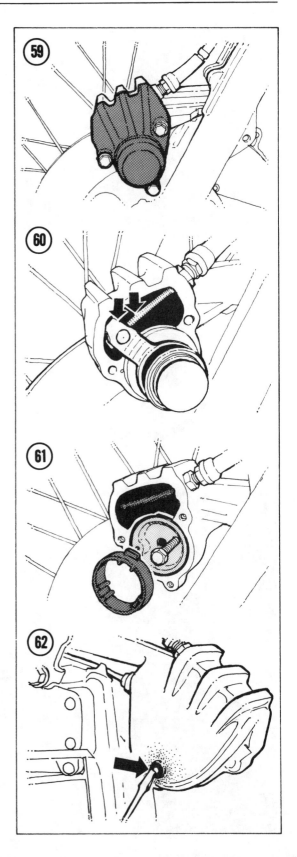

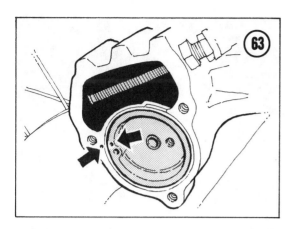

14. Install the ratchet and check its operation.

15. Install the brake arm and caliper cover.

NOTE: *Always use a new gasket.*

16. To ensure full brake lever release, loosen the adjusting bolt fully, then turn it in all the way. Finally, back it out 2 to 3 turns, and tighten the locknut.

17. Operate the front brake hand lever 10-12 times (the brake will adjust itself).

18. Rotate the front wheel to be sure that the brake does not drag.

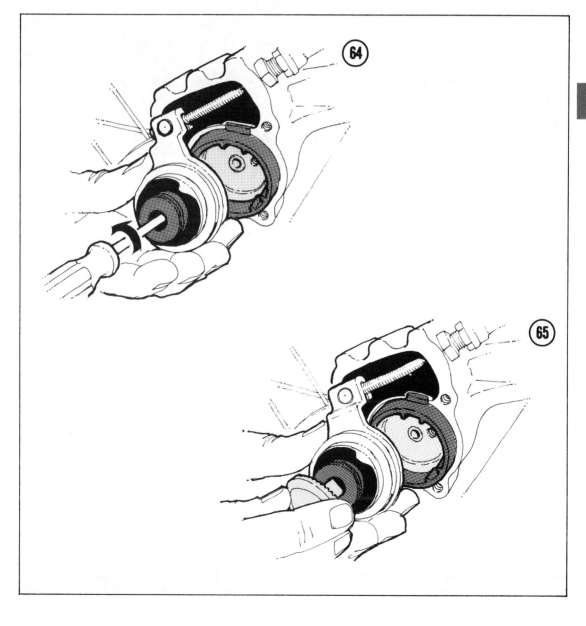

Front Disc Brake Adjustment (Mechanically-Actuated)

The front disc brake is self-adjusting and needs no periodic maintenance other than brake pad replacement.

Front (Drum) Brake Adjustment

To adjust the front drum brake, refer to **Figure 66**.

1. Support the motorcycle so that its front wheel is free to turn.
2. Loosen locknut.
3. Turn adjuster nut to obtain desired braking action.
4. Tighten locknut.

Rear (Drum) Brake Adjustment

The rear drum brake is operated by a rod. Simply turn the adjusting nut (**Figure 67**) until the rear brake pedal has approximately ¾-1 in. (20-25mm) of free play (**Figure 68**).

REAR SUSPENSION

Major rear suspension components are 2 shock absorbers, 2 springs, and a swinging arm.

Shock Absorbers and Springs

The rear shock absorbers are not serviceable, and must be replaced in the event of malfunction, as follows.

1. Remove shock absorber mounting bolts (**Figure 69**) and pull shock absorbers off.
2. Compress the shock absorber with a special spring compressor as shown in **Figure 70**, until the spring seat can be removed. Then release pressure from the tool.
3. To install the new shock absorbers, reverse the preceding steps.

Swinging Arm

The pivot section of the swinging arm is susceptible to wear, especially in the shaft and bushings. Replace the pivot shaft if it is bent more than 0.02 in. (0.5mm). Replace bushings and/or shaft if the clearance between them exceeds 0.014 in. (0.35mm).

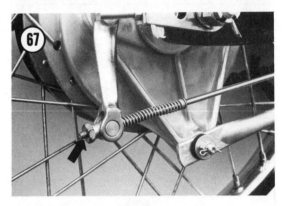

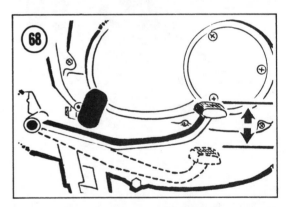

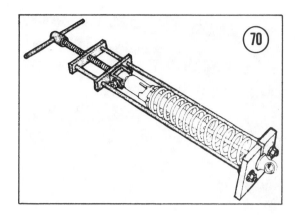

Disassemble the swinging arm and grease its pivot shaft and bushings every 6,000 miles (9,000 kilometers). Refer to **Figure 71** for the following procedure:

1. Remove hex nut, washer, and dust seal cap.

2. Slide pivot bolt out of center collar.

3. Remove center collar; grease inside of the pivot bushing; inside and outside of center collar; and outside of pivot bolt.

4. Assemble by reversing the preceding steps.

DRIVE CHAIN

The drive chain becomes worn after prolonged use. Wear in pins, bushings, and rollers causes chain stretch. Sliding action between roller surfaces and sprocket teeth also contribute to wear.

Cleaning and Adjustment

1. Disconnect the master link (**Figure 72**) and remove chain.

2. Clean chain thoroughly with solvent.

3. Rinse chain with clean solvent, then blow dry with compressed air.

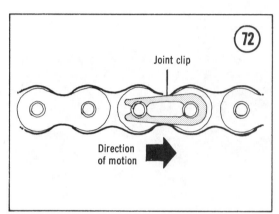

Joint clip

Direction of motion

7

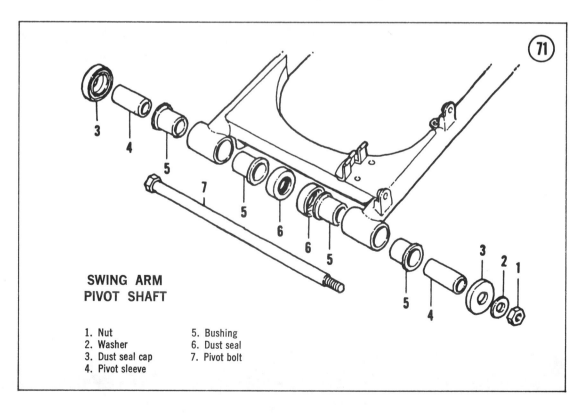

SWING ARM PIVOT SHAFT

1. Nut	5. Bushing
2. Washer	6. Dust seal
3. Dust seal cap	7. Pivot bolt
4. Pivot sleeve	

4. Examine chain carefully for wear or damage. Replace if there is any doubt as to its condition. If chain is okay, lubricate by soaking in oil, or any of the special chain lubricants available in any motorcycle shop.

5. Install the chain. Be sure that the master link is installed as shown in **Figure 72**.

6. Refer to **Figure 73**. Proceed with chain adjustment, as follows:

   a. Remove the cotter pin and loosen the rear axle nut.

   b. Loosen locknut on each side.

   c. There is one adjustment bolt on each side. Turn it until there is ¾-1 in. (20-25mm) of up-and-down movement in the center of the lower chain run (**Figure 74**).

   d. Be sure that the reference marks on the swinging arm and the index mark on the chain adjuster (refer to **Figure 73**) are in the same relative positions on each side.

7. Tighten the rear axle nut, then install a new cotter pin (refer to **Figure 73**).

8. Adjust the rear brake (refer to *Brakes* section, this chapter).

INDEX

8

NOTES

NOTES

MAINTENANCE LOG

Date	Miles	Type of Service

BMW

M308	500 & 600 CC Twins, 55-69
M309	F650, 1994-2000
M500-3	BMW K-Series, 85-97
M502-3	BMW R50/5-R100 GSPD, 70-96
M503-2	R850, R1100, R1150 and R1200C, 93-04

HARLEY-DAVIDSON

M419	Sportsters, 59-85
M428	Sportster Evolution, 86-90
M429-4	Sportster Evolution, 91-03
M418	Panheads, 48-65
M420	Shovelheads, 66-84
M421-3	FLS/FXS Evolution, 84-99
M423	FLS/FXS Twin Cam 88B, 2000-2003
M422	FLH/FLT/FXR Evolution, 84-94
M430-2	FLH/FLT Twin Cam 88, 1999-2003
M424-2	FXD Evolution, 91-98
M425-2	FXD Twin Cam, 99-03

HONDA

ATVs

M316	Odyssey FL250, 77-84
M311	ATC, TRX & Fourtrax 70-125, 70-87
M433	Fourtrax 90 ATV, 93-00
M326	ATC185 & 200, 80-86
M347	ATC200X & Fourtrax 200SX, 86-88
M455	ATC250 & Fourtrax 200/ 250, 84-87
M342	ATC250R, 81-84
M348	TRX250R/Fourtrax 250R & ATC250R, 85-89
M456-3	TRX250X 87-92; TRX300EX 93-04
M446	TRX250 Recon 97-02
M346-3	TRX300/Fourtrax 300 & TRX300FW/Fourtrax 4x4, 88-00
M200	TRX350 Rancher, 00-03
M459-3	TRX400 Foreman 95-03
M454-2	TRX400EX 99-03
M205	TRX450 Foreman, 98-04

Singles

M310-13	50-110cc OHC Singles, 65-99
M319	XR50R-XR70R, 97-03
M315	100-350cc OHC, 69-82
M317	Elsinore, 125-250cc, 73-80
M442	CR60-125R Pro-Link, 81-88
M431-2	CR80R, 89-95, CR125R, 89-91
M435	CR80, 96-02
M457-2	CR125R & CR250R, 92-97
M464	CR125R, 1998-2002
M443	CR250R-500R Pro-Link, 81-87
M432-3	CR250R, 88-91 & CR500R, 88-01
M437	CR250R, 97-01
M312-13	XL/XR75-100, 75-03
M318-4	XL/XR/TLR 125-200, 79-03
M328-4	XL/XR250, 78-00; XL/XR350R 83-85; XR200R, 84-85; XR250L, 91-96
M320-2	XR400R, 96-04
M339-7	XL/XR 500-650, 79-03

Twins

M321	125-200cc, 65-78
M322	250-350cc, 64-74
M323	250-360cc Twins, 74-77
M324-5	Twinstar, Rebel 250 & Nighthawk 250, 78-03
M334	400-450cc, 78-87
M333	450 & 500cc, 65-76
M335	CX & GL500/650 Twins, 78-83
M344	VT500, 83-88
M313	VT700 & 750, 83-87
M314	VT750C Shadow, 98-03
M440	VT1100C Shadow, 85-96
M460-3	VT1100C Series, 95-04

Fours

M332	CB350-550cc, SOHC, 71-78
M345	CB550 & 650, 83-85
M336	CB650, 79-82
M341	CB750 SOHC, 69-78
M337	CB750 DOHC, 79-82
M436	CB750 Nighthawk, 91-93 & 95-99
M325	CB900, 1000 & 1100, 80-83
M439	Hurricane 600, 87-90
M441-2	CBR600, 91-98
M445	CBR600F4, 99-03
M434	CBR900RR Fireblade, 93-98
M329	500cc V-Fours, 84-86
M438	Honda VFR800, 98-00
M349	700-1000 Interceptor, 83-85
M458-2	VFR700F-750F, 86-97
M327	700-1100cc V-Fours, 82-88
M340	GL1000 & 1100, 75-83
M504	GL1200, 84-87
M508	ST1100/PAN European, 90-02

Sixes

M505	GL1500 Gold Wing, 88-92
M506-2	GL1500 Gold Wing, 93-00
M507	GL1800 Gold Wing, 01-04
M462-2	GL1500C Valkyrie, 97-03

KAWASAKI

ATVs

M465-2	KLF220 & KLF250 Bayou, 88-03
M466-3	KLF300 Bayou, 86-04
M467	KLF400 Bayou, 93-99
M470	KEF300 Lakota, 95-99
M385	KSF250 Mojave, 87-00

Singles

M350-9	Rotary Valve 80-350cc, 66-01
M444-2	KX60, 83-02; KX80 83-90
M448	KX80/85/100, 89-03
M351	KDX200, 83-88
M447-2	KX125 & KX250, 82-91 KX500, 83-02
M472-2	KX125, 92-00
M473-2	KX250, 92-00
M474	KLR650, 87-03

Twins

M355	KZ400, KZ/Z440, EN450 & EN500, 74-95
M360-3	EX500, GPZ500S, Ninja R, 87-02
M356-3	Vulcan 700 & 750, 85-04
M354-2	Vulcan 800 & Vulcan 800 Classic, 95-04
M357-2	Vulcan 1500, 87-99
M471-2	Vulcan Classic 1500, 96-04

Fours

M449	KZ500/550 & ZX550, 79-85
M450	KZ, Z & ZX750, 80-85
M358	KZ650, 77-83
M359-3	900-1000cc Fours, 73-81
M451-3	1000 &1100cc Fours, 81-02
M452-3	ZX500 & 600 Ninja, 85-97
M453-3	Ninja ZX900-1100 84-01
M468	ZX6 Ninja, 90-97
M469	ZX7 Ninja, 91-98
M453-3	900-1100 Ninja, 84-01
M409	Concours, 86-04

POLARIS

ATVs

M496	Polaris ATV, 85-95
M362	Polaris Magnum ATV, 96-98
M363	Scrambler 500, 4X4 97-00
M365-2	Sportsman/Xplorer, 96-03

SUZUKI

ATVs

M381	ALT/LT 125 & 185, 83-87
M475	LT230 & LT250, 85-90
M380-2	LT250R Quad Racer, 85-92
M343	LTF500F Quadrunner, 98-00
M483-2	Suzuki King Quad/ Quad Runner 250, 87-98

Singles

M371	RM50-400 Twin Shock, 75-81
M369	125-400cc 64-81
M379	RM125-500 Single Shock, 81-88
M476	DR250-350, 90-94
M384-2	LS650 Savage, 86-03
M386	RM80-250, 89-95
M400	RM125, 96-00
M401	RM250, 96-02

Twins

M372	GS400-450 Twins, 77-87
M481-4	VS700-800 Intruder, 85-04
M482-2	VS1400 Intruder, 87-01
M484-3	GS500E Twins, 89-02
M361	SV650, 1999-2002

Triple

M368	380-750cc, 72-77

Fours

M373	GS550, 77-86
M364	GS650, 81-83
M370	GS750 Fours, 77-82
M376	GS850-1100 Shaft Drive, 79-84
M378	GS1100 Chain Drive, 80-81
M383-3	Katana 600, 88-96 GSX-R750-1100, 86-87
M331	GSX-R600, 97-00
M478-2	GSX-R750, 88-92 GSX750F Katana, 89-96
M485	GSX-R750, 96-99
M338	GSF600 Bandit, 95-00
M353	GSF1200 Bandit, 96-03

YAMAHA

ATVs

M499	YFM80 Badger, 85-01
M394	YTM/YFM200 & 225, 83-86
M488-4	Blaster, 88-02
M489-2	Timberwolf, 89-00
M487-5	Warrior, 87-04
M486-5	Banshee, 87-04
M490-2	YFM350 Moto-4 & Big Bear, 87-98
M493	YFM400FW Kodiak, 93-98
M280	Raptor 660R, 01-03

Singles

M492-2	PW50 & PW80, BW80 Big Wheel 80, 81-02
M410	80-175 Piston Port, 68-76
M415	250-400cc Piston Port, 68-76
M412	DT & MX 100-400, 77-83
M414	IT125-490, 76-86
M393	YZ50-80 Monoshock, 78-90
M413	YZ100-490 Monoshock, 76-84
M390	YZ125-250, 85-87 YZ490, 85-90
M391	YZ125-250, 88-93 WR250Z, 91-93
M497-2	YZ125, 94-01
M498	YZ250, 94-98 and WR250Z, 94-97
M406	YZ250F & WR250F, 01-03
M491-2	YZ400F, YZ426F, WR400F WR426F, 98-02
M417	XT125-250, 80-84
M480-3	XT/TT 350, 85-00
M405	XT500 & TT500, 76-81
M416	XT/TT 600, 83-89

Twins

M403	650cc, 70-82
M395-10	XV535-1100 Virago, 81-03
M495-3	V-Star 650, 98-04
M281	V-Star 1100, 99-04

Triple

M404	XS750 & 850, 77-81

Fours

M387	XJ550, XJ600 & FJ600, 81-92
M494	XJ600 Seca II, 92-98
M388	YX600 Radian & FZ600, 86-90
M396	FZR600, 89-93
M392	FZ700-750 & Fazer, 85-87
M411	XS1100 Fours, 78-81
M397	FJ1100 & 1200, 84-93
M375	V-Max, 85-03
M374	Royal Star, 96-03
M461	YZF-R6, 99-04
M398	YZF-R1, 98-03

VINTAGE MOTORCYCLES

Clymer® Collection Series

M330	Vintage British Street Bikes, BSA, 500–650cc Unit Twins; Norton, 750 & 850cc Commandos; Triumph, 500-750cc Twins
M300	Vintage Dirt Bikes, V. 1 Bultaco, 125-370cc Singles; Montesa, 123-360cc Singles; Ossa, 125-250cc Singles
M301	Vintage Dirt Bikes, V. 2 CZ, 125-400cc Singles; Husqvarna, 125-450cc Singles; Maico, 250-501cc Singles; Hodaka, 90-125cc Singles
M305	Vintage Japanese Street Bikes Honda, 250 & 305cc Twins; Kawasaki, 250-750cc Triples; Kawasaki, 900 & 1000cc Fours